Al

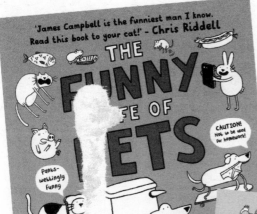

'Deliciously delightful.
Superbly epic and funnier
than any other book
I've read.'

Ethan, aged 9

'I enjoyed ___ ery bit
of it. I thin' ___ t anyone
who reads ___ 'll laugh
their ___ off
(much ___ did).'

Em ___ 10

THE
FUNNY
LIFE OF
TEACHERS

Face-
achingly
Funny!

CAUTION!
Not to be used
for homework!

HELP!

JAMES
CAMPBELL

ROB
JONES

Will make you laugh so much snot
will fly out of your nose

BLOOMSBURY

Really good at homework
(if the homework is drawing
dogs on skateboards)

For Ben – James Campbell

**For my Grandma, Lily. Celebrating her
100th birthday this year – Rob Jones**

BLOOMSBURY CHILDREN'S BOOKS
Bloomsbury Publishing Plc
50 Bedford Square, London, WC1B 3DP, UK
29 Earlsfort Terrace, Dublin 2, Ireland

BLOOMSBURY, BLOOMSBURY CHILDREN'S BOOKS and the Diana logo
are trademarks of Bloomsbury Publishing Plc
First published in Great Britain 2020 by Bloomsbury Publishing Plc
Text copyright © James Campbell, 2020
Illustrations copyright © Rob Jones, 2020

A catalogue record for this book is available from the British Library

ISBN: PB: 978-1-5266-1549-7 eBook: 978-1-5266-2540-3

4 6 8 10 9 7 5

Printed and bound in Great Britain by CPI (UK) Ltd, Croydon CR0 4YY

MIX
Paper | Supporting
responsible forestry
FSC® C171272
FSC
www.fsc.org

To find out more about our authors and books visit www.bloomsbu...
and sign up for our newsletters

The author and publisher recommend enabling SafeSearch when using the Internet in... ...n with
this book. We can accept no responsibility for information published on the Int...

THE
FUNNY
LIFE OF
SHARKS

JAMES
CAMPBELL

ROB
JONES

BLOOMSBURY
CHILDREN'S BOOKS

LONDON OXFORD NEW YORK NEW DELHI SYDNEY

Read this before you dare go any further . . .

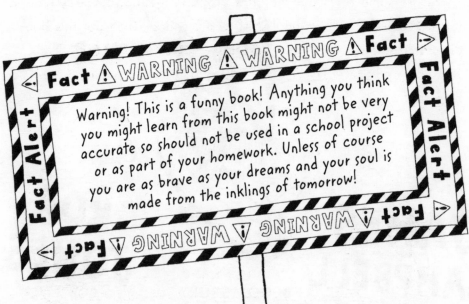

WHAT SORT OF BOOK IS THIS?

This is NOT a normal book.

This is **not** some sort of fact book. It's not a reference book. There are some facts but they are probably wrong. If you're looking for **proper** educational stuff about sharks, then put this book down immediately and **run away screaming**. If it's practical and useful information you want I can recommend the following books:

I'm Every Woman: A history of feminism in the shark world — Sharka Khan

Facts About Sharks — Finn Hammerhead

The Serious Life of the Ocean — Frugal Sharkish

This book is for four types of people:

1. People who really like sharks, are fascinated by sharks, and think sharks are fantastic. You just **love love LOVE sharks sharks SHARKS!**

2. People who don't like sharks at all. Maybe you are afraid of sharks? Maybe you have **nightmares** about sharks? Maybe every time you step into a room for the first time you look around in the corners and on the ceiling to check that there are no sharks? Don't worry – this book will help with all of that. Or make it **much, much worse.**

3. People who **ARE sharks**. Or maybe you are a **shark-person** (half person, half shark). Or just a shark who has taught itself to read from looking at the writing on all the plastic packaging in the sea? This book might help you learn more about people!

4. **P**eople who have **literally no interest** in sharks at all. Don't care about sharks. Find sharks boring. Never even heard of sharks. Think sharks are for other sorts of people but not you. You are more interested in other things that no one has written a book about, like picking out your bogeys and arranging them in alphabetical order; making a slide show about a weird dream you had about being a bat; or maybe just playing computer games for so long that your eyes have started to bleed and you've forgotten how to talk in anything but memes and wibble. **BUT** – despite all this: you really like laughing and giggling and **fart-chuckling*** until your shoes fly off and distract a police officer from his regular duties!

* Fart-chuckling is when you chuckle so much that you accidentally fart.

7

This is not a normal book

Before you go any further I really should warn you that this is not a normal book. **Not normal at all.**

You read a normal book by starting off on **page ONE**. Then you turn the page and read **page TWO**. And then **page THREE**. And you carry on like that until you get to the end of the book, and then you say 'hooray' and have a biscuit.

It would be weird, wouldn't it, if you read a book by starting with **a random page** in the middle of the book?

Hooray.

First I shall read page 85. And next I will read the last page, and then the first page. And now I shall read page 99 because it is my favourite number.

I ♥ reading books properly

Well, the book you're holding in your twinkly little hands at the moment **IS THAT KIND OF WEIRD!!!**

You can read the pages of this book in any order you like. You can read it forwards or backwards or even sideways. Probably the most fun way is to **follow the signposts**. If you like the sound of finding out more about something, just go to that page. You might then go back to where you started or you might see something else as you're flicking through.

There is no **WRONG** way to read this book.

Apart from reading it while robbing a bank, using the money to buy illegal uranium, and then holding the world to ransom for a **GAZILLION DOLLARS**. That would be wrong.

If you can think of any other **WRONG** ways to read this book, please feel free to let me know by emailing: idontreallycare@whatever.com

What this book is about

This book is about sharks. So what are sharks?

Well, there are two answers to this. The **scientific answer** and the **silly answer**.

THE SCIENTIFIC ANSWER IS:

A shark is a member of the **elasmobranch fish family** characterised by a cartilaginous skeleton, gills on the side and pectoral fins that are not fused to the head.

AND THE SILLY ANSWER IS:

A shark is a pointy-nosed, fishy-fin swimmer with big teeth and **weird eyes**.

A warning about facts

Occasionally, this book will give you some **actual facts**.

For example: Sharks have to keep moving forwards, otherwise they die.

But actually NOT ALL sharks have to keep moving forwards. Nurse sharks sleep for hours and hours every day, just sitting on the bottom of the sea.

You have to be very **careful** with facts. In 25 years' time, if you read this book to your children, you will find that half of the facts in this book are **WRONG**. The stories, the jokes and the sillies, however, will still be true until Jupiter pops out of its orbit and wanders over to Neptune for a game of cricket.

Snot-trousers!

Schmillet

Pagging taggers!

Tagging paggers!

Death and rude words

Now, in order to write a book about sharks (even

Ankle-grazers

a funny one), I have to write about some fairly scary things.
And I might have to use words like **DIE, ATTACK, KILL,
MASSACRE, SLAUGHTER, ARMAGEDDON and
NERVOUSUNDERWATERBLOWOFF.**

Thumb-trap

If you are the sort of person that gets upset
by words like this, then this book probably
isn't for you.

Wum-trap

Flum-trap

As well as scary death words,
the other thing I will need to do in
this book is use some rude words.
But this book will not contain any
rude words that you might have
seen or heard before. It will contain

Crumbling plimpturtles!

lots of rude words and phrases that no one has ever seen or
heard before like:

I'm-sorry-that-number-has-not-been-recognised

Grouting-sticks!

Nipple

Fart-lover

Stouting-gricks!

What the hoppernickers do you think you're blinging doing,
you crab-worrying etch-a-sketch!

13

Beginning page

Welcome to the beginning of the book. And well done for making it this far! Some people don't make it to this page without deciding that words are just far too complicated for them and they'd have a much better time spending a couple of hours flipping a bottle, staring at a banana or laughing at their own reflection in a spoon.

This, then, is where **The Funny Life of Sharks** REALLY starts. Here are loads of signposts to get you going. Choose one that sounds interesting and go to that page!

What are sharks?: Page 16

Are you afraid of sharks?: Page 24

Shark teeth: Page 28

TV shows about sharks: Page 36

How do sharks navigate?: Page 80

Shark skin: Page 92

Shark eyes: Page 119

Why is there so much plastic in the sea?: Page 130

Different sharks/ different food: Page 142

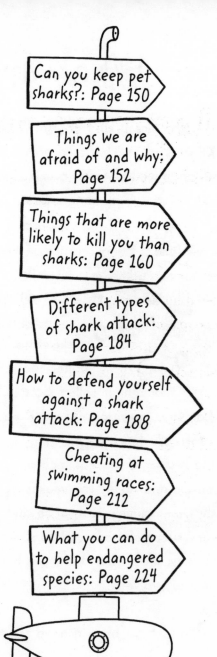

Can you keep pet sharks?: Page 150

Things we are afraid of and why: Page 152

Things that are more likely to kill you than sharks: Page 160

Different types of shark attack: Page 184

How to defend yourself against a shark attack: Page 188

Cheating at swimming races: Page 212

What you can do to help endangered species: Page 224

What are sharks?

Sharks are a kind of fish. There are over **500 different types** of shark. Some are so tiny you could fit one on an individual-sized pizza. Others are bigger than a bus.

The main thing that makes a shark different from being just a bitey type of fish is their skeletons. Fish skeletons are made out of bone. Shark skeletons, however, are made from something called **cartilage**, which is the same thing that your ears and nose are made of. Cartilage is strong but it's also really flexible and light.

The rest of a shark is mainly muscle and teeth. This makes sharks extremely fast, agile and very successful as predators. And so they should be: they have had a very long time to evolve ...

Sharks have been around for **450 million years**.

That's **450,000,000 years**.

How do sharks navigate?: Page 80

That's very old.

Think of it this way: our **ANCIENT ancestors** have only been around for 6,000,000 years. And people like you and me have only been around for about 200,000 years.

Compared to sharks, we are babies.

Shark skin: Page 92

There were sharks swimming in the oceans when there were dinosaurs on the planet.

Some of the most interesting things about sharks are their teeth, their skin, their love of opera and the way they navigate.

Shark teeth: Page 28

Famous types of shark

There are loads of different sharks but the most famous ones are the ones that look really **scary** and have a reputation for biting people. You might have heard of some of the following:

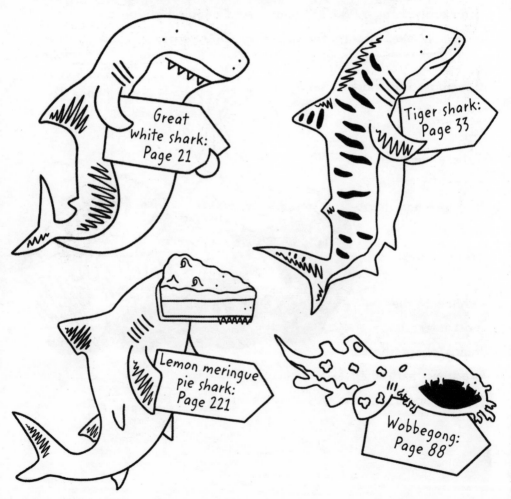

Great white shark: Page 21

Tiger shark: Page 33

Lemon meringue pie shark: Page 221

Wobbegong: Page 88

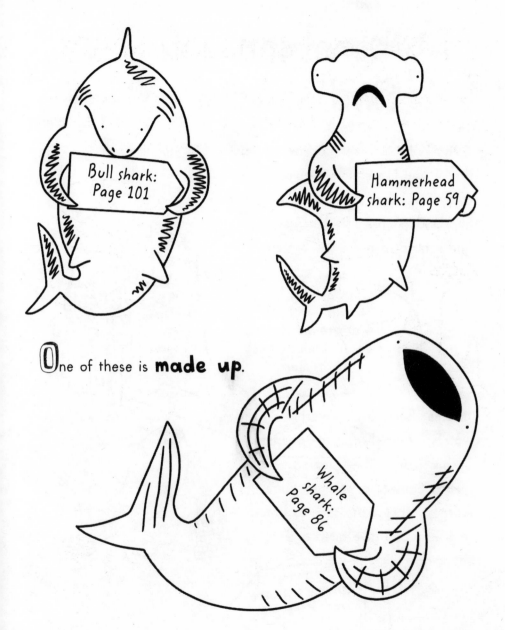

Bull shark:
Page 101

Hammerhead
shark: Page 59

One of these is **made up**.

Whale
shark:
Page 86

Where can you find sharks?

How do sharks navigate?: Page 80

Sharks live in every ocean on Earth. That means that if you like sharks, you're never that far away from one. Unless you're in a lift. Sharks don't use lifts because they find it hard to press the buttons.

Could you press Lower Ground for me, please? I haven't got any fingers.

Some sharks live in warm waters, others live in the deepest oceans among the freezing gloom. Some sharks make huge journeys across the seas to breed and feed and give birth and go shopping.

How many seas are there?: Page 146

Great white shark

This is probably one of the most famous of sharks, mainly due to the film **Jaws**.

Great whites live in all the oceans, usually in the cooler bits and near to the coast.

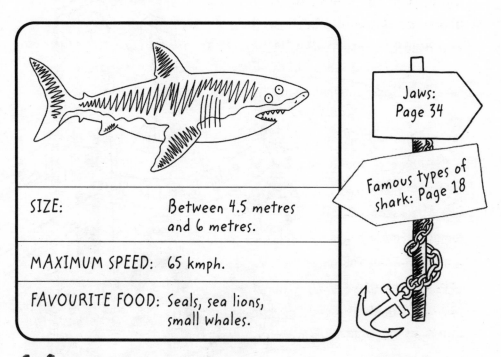

SIZE: Between 4.5 metres and 6 metres.

MAXIMUM SPEED: 65 kmph.

FAVOURITE FOOD: Seals, sea lions, small whales.

Jaws: Page 34

Famous types of shark: Page 18

Why are they called great whites? Because the underside of them is white. And they are great.

Are you afraid of sharks?: Page 24

How far away from sharks can I get?

If you don't like sharks, and you want to be as far away from them as possible, you should be as **far away** from the sea as possible.

If you live in the UK, the furthest away you can get from the sea is a village called Coton-in-the-Elms in Derbyshire. People who live here are 113 kilometres away from the sea (and sharks).

Coton-in-the-Elms is the home of the 'We Really Don't Like Sharks Society'. Members meet once a month in the village pub, so they can be as far away from sharks as possible.

My phobia of sharks: Page 82

22

If you want to get as far away from the ocean as possible and still be on Planet Earth, then you should go to the **Dzungarian Basin**, which is in the Xingjiang Uygur province of China. If you stand there, you will be 2,647 kilometres away from the sea.

Children who live here do not go on day trips to the **seaside**. It would take them about a week to get there!

The Dzungarian Basin is a great place to live if you are afraid of sharks and/or deckchairs.

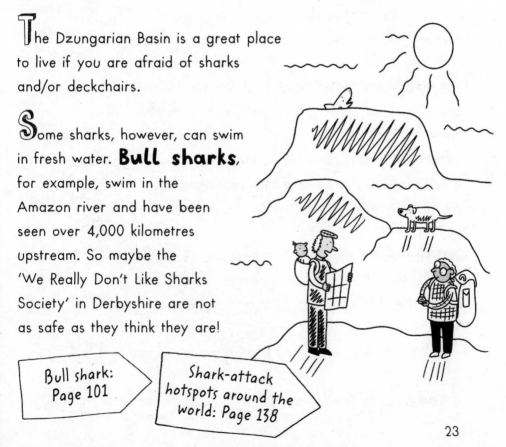

Some sharks, however, can swim in fresh water. **Bull sharks**, for example, swim in the Amazon river and have been seen over 4,000 kilometres upstream. So maybe the 'We Really Don't Like Sharks Society' in Derbyshire are not as safe as they think they are!

Bull shark: Page 101

Shark-attack hotspots around the world: Page 138

Are you afraid of sharks?

I did a survey of nearly 1,000 children in various primary schools around East Anglia where I live.

Utterly **terrified** of sharks (They are everywhere and they are out to get me!) - **4%**

My best friend is a shark: Page 126

Afraid of sharks (I don't like swimming in the ocean because I worry I will get eaten) - **44%**

Wary of sharks (They are quite bitey, aren't they? And they have big teeth. Probably best to stay away from them) - **36%**

Neutral towards sharks (I have literally never bothered to think about what I think about sharks. I'm going back to looking in my spoon now) - **1%**

I **like** sharks (I wish I had a shark as my friend) - **13%**

I **love** sharks (I want one to be my best friend forever) - **2%**

LOVE Terrified Neutral Like Afraid Wary

Are you still afraid of sharks?

So according to my survey, most people have **negative feelings** towards sharks.

I then asked all the negative people if they had ever met a shark.

None of them.

Absolutely none of them had ever met a shark.

The only people in the whole survey who had met a shark (while scuba diving in a shark experience at an aquarium) were the ones who wanted to have one as a best friend forever!

So this suggests to me that people who have never met a shark tend to be afraid of them. But if people get to see them up close, they find that actually sharks are really fascinating, interesting, awe-inspiring, **loveable** creatures!

Throw him to the sharks.

Yay! I love sharks.

JAWS

Bee nice: Page 30

Swimming with sharks: Page 232

25

I needed to find out more about sharks

I decided that I needed to find out more about sharks. And this decision filled me with **excitement** and **nervousness** all at the same time.

I began to think about these questions:

- Why was I afraid of sharks?
- What is so scary about sharks anyway?
- Have people always been afraid of sharks?
- Where have all my socks gone?
- Are sharks afraid of us?
- Seriously, where have all my socks gone?
- How many people actually get bitten by a shark?
- I'm always buying socks and yet I have no idea where any of them are!
- Where have all my pagging socks gone?

How many people get eaten by sharks?: Page 51

Then I realised that my only experience of sharks was what I had seen at the movies and on the television. I am one of the people who had **never** met a shark.

TV shows about sharks: Page 36

And most people have never met a shark, because you don't tend to see them wandering around your local supermarket, do you?

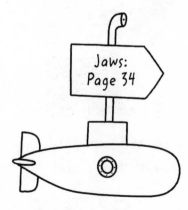

Jaws: Page 34

Shark teeth

Sharks have about **450 teeth** in up to seven rows. They can go through about 30,000 teeth in a lifetime. The shark tooth fairy is very busy.

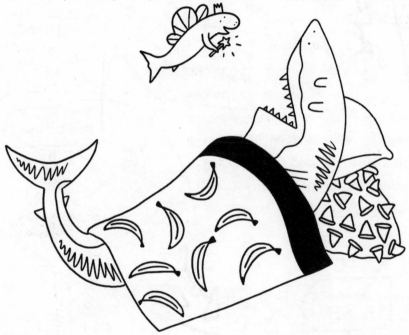

Sharks grow their teeth in a kind of conveyor-belt system, so they are always falling out and more just grow in their place.

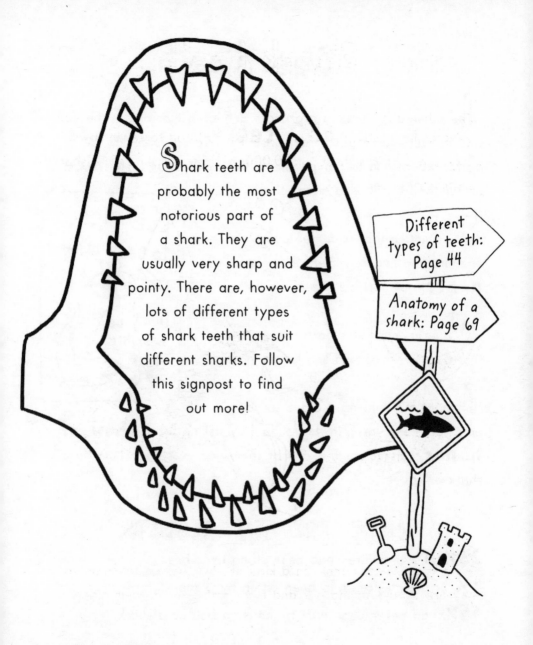

$\mathcal{S}$hark teeth are probably the most notorious part of a shark. They are usually very sharp and pointy. There are, however, lots of different types of shark teeth that suit different sharks. Follow this signpost to find out more!

Different types of teeth: Page 44

Anatomy of a shark: Page 69

Bee nice

The other day I was in a primary school in Norfolk. In the hall, on the wall, was a poster designed by a seven-year-old. The poster was trying to get people to think about **being nice** rather than horrible to each other.

You'll notice that what the poster is encouraging children to do is be nice like **a bee**, not horrible like a shark.

Whoever made this poster must think that bees are nice and sharks are horrible.

BEE nice to each other.
Don't be horrible.

This got me thinking. I did a survey of all of the children in that school by asking for a **show of hands**. I asked them if any of them had ever been hurt by a shark or a bee.

HERE ARE THE RESULTS:

23% of the children had been stung by a bee.

1% of the children had been bitten by a shark.

45% had never been hurt by either a bee or a shark.

30

Making things up just to sound funny: Page 182

12% didn't really understand the question.

2% were asleep.

3% were not in the room because they were doing an after-lunch poo.

Things we are afraid of and why: Page 152

§o, only one child had been hurt by a shark. And when I questioned him properly it turned out that he hadn't actually been bitten by a shark at all. In fact, he had never even seen a shark and had been making the whole thing up just to sound funny.

You are a quinkelling schmillet!

§o it would seem that in general, children think sharks are **scary** even though they have no actual experience of being hurt by a shark. Not even with words.

31

Moving forwards: Page 40

Shark teeth: Page 28

Do sharks sleep?: Page 78

TV shows about sharks: Page 36

What's so scary about sharks?

I have asked lots of children, and some grown-ups, what it is that is so scary about sharks and most of them said, **'It's all those teeth!'**

Other people have mentioned the **cold dead eyes** and the fact that sharks are always moving and don't sleep.

Of course, you don't have to meet a shark to get some feelings about them. We see sharks all the time on the television and in films and cartoons. And, usually, they are portrayed as being really dangerous and scary. There is normally scary music playing. And they are often showing everyone their massive teeth ...

Nice shark films: Page 120

Tiger shark

Baby **tiger sharks** have black stripes all over them but as they get bigger the stripes fade away. On an adult tiger shark the stripes are almost invisible so they don't look like tigers at all.

How do sharks navigate: Page 80

Different sharks/different foods: Page 142

Ten things you didn't know about sharks: Page 205

Famous types of shark: Page 18

SIZE: Between 3 and 4 metres long.

FAVOURITE FOOD: Dolphins, fish, turtles, dugongs.

THIRD FUN FACT: Tiger sharks are usually solitary except when mating (it's difficult to do that on your own).

EXTRA FUN FACT: They migrate thousands of kilometres to get to warmer waters.

33

Jaws

In 1975 the most iconic shark movie came out. It was based on Peter Benchley's book and it had a **huge effect** on the world.

In the story, a sleepy little island gets visited by a monster-sized great white shark with a massive appetite for people.

For the first half of the film you hardly see the shark. Apparently when they started filming, it took them ages to get the **shark robot** they were using to work properly so they had to film bits with people just splashing in the water. The thing is, this actually made the film scarier because there is nothing more powerful than your own imagination.

Where is your imagination?: Page 43

This film really started to make the world afraid of sharks. If the film had been about some weird monster dinosaur, it wouldn't have had the same effect.

I watched the film when I was 12 years old and it was the first time I'd ever really thought about shark attacks and how scary they were.

In his later years, Peter Benchley said that he wished he had never written **Jaws**, and became a passionate supporter of sharks in the wild, campaigning against shark finning and for the protection of these amazing animals.

Shark finning: Page 64

One of the most memorable things about the film **Jaws** is the **music**. It sounds like what you say if your mum has asked if you've done your homework.

'Done it. Done it. Done it done it done it done it. Done it.'

Nice shark films: Page 120

Negative language used to describe sharks: Page 180

TV shows about sharks

The other day I was watching the TV and I stumbled upon a programme called simply **Sharks!!!** The programme started with lots of shots of massive sharks snapping around and looking scary.

Then the voiceover started:

'Sharks are really SCARY. But you are more likely to be struck by lightning than you are to be attacked by a shark.'

Great. From that point on I was also afraid of being struck by lightning.

But the TV voiceover carried on:

'You are more likely to be struck by lightning than you are to be attacked by a shark. Unless you are a seal.'

A funny story about voiceovers: Page 144

And then it cut to a film of a seal bobbing about in the water, and then a massive shark popped up from nowhere and ate the seal in a fairly **dramatic** teeth-first, seal-in-pieces kind of way.

But what would happen if a SEAL saw that TV programme?

You're probably thinking, 'Seals don't watch TV. There are no TVs in the ocean.'

Well, maybe there are. People are always going on about how much **plastic** there is in the ocean. Maybe there are some televisions as well!

Why is there so much plastic in the sea?: Page 130

How many seas are there?: Page 146

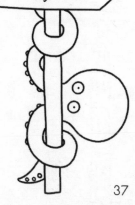

37

TV shows for seals

Imagine that somewhere out in the ocean, there is a colony of seals living on a bunch of rocks.

And they've found an old television that no one wants any more. One of those boxy ones from the last millennium that your grandma has got in the spare bedroom.

Collective nouns: Page 148

I've written this bit as a play:

[MUMMY SEAL AND BABY SEAL ARE WATCHING TV]

BABY SEAL: Ooh, Mummy, there's a programme on the telly about sharks.

MUMMY SEAL: Ooh. How exciting.

TV VOICEOVER: Sharks are very scary.

A funny story about voiceovers: Page 144

BABY SEAL: They do look scary, don't they, Mummy? Look at their big teeth. Have you ever seen a shark, Mummy?

MUMMY SEAL: Yes, maybe. I think so. Your Auntie Gwen met a shark once.

BABY SEAL: Who's Auntie Gwen?

TV VOICEOVER: But you are more likely to be struck by lightning than you are to be attacked by a shark.

BABY SEAL: Ooh. That's all right then.

MUMMY SEAL: Don't worry, love. You're quite safe.

TV VOICEOVER: Unless you are a seal. Chomp chomp. Munch. Aaaaaargggggghhhh. Gulp.

[BABY SEAL STARES AT THE TV FOR A MOMENT AND THEN LOOKS AT MUMMY SEAL]

BABY SEAL: (With trembling lips) Mummy?

MUMMY SEAL: Yes, love?

BABY SEAL: Am I a seal?

MUMMY SEAL: Yes, love. You are a seal. Sorry about that.

The Lightning Channel: Page 46

Things that should not be in this book: Page 236

BABY SEAL: Oh, snot-trousers!

Moving forwards

Most sharks **never sleep** because they have to have water continually flowing over their gills or they will die.

Gills are the fish equivalent of lungs. There's no point having lungs if you are a fish, as every time you breathed in, you'd drown. Water is also called H_2O, which means it is made from hydrogen and oxygen. And gills can extract oxygen from water.

I asked the University of Plymouth's Marine Biology Department why other fish can stay still and keep breathing but most sharks have to keep swimming along.

A lovely man called Ben Ciotto said that the bits in gills that get the oxygen out of water are called **'filaments'**. In non-shark fish, these filaments are sort of glued together in pairs. So they're better at getting oxygen from water than shark gills. Also, fish jaws are really clever, and fish can make water flow across their gills without actually going anywhere.

Sometimes when I'm in the bath, I suck up water and spit it over my shoulder while singing, 'I'm a fishy-wishy fishy, I'm a fishy-wishy fish.' Why don't you try doing this and see how long it takes for your mum to shout at you?

Nurse sharks are one of the few sharks that can stay still without drowning. They spend most of their time sitting around on the bottom of the ocean. They are called **nurse sharks** because they are used in hospitals as a way of keeping patients quiet.

Moving forwards is also one of the most annoying phrases people use.

So moving forwards, can we agree to improve our behaviour?

Do sharks sleep?: Page 78

Why are you saying 'moving forwards'? It's not like you have any choice. Unless you have a time machine, you're always going to be moving forwards.

Moving backwards, I wish that I hadn't tried to wee on the ceiling.

The Grammarhead Shark: Page 158

Daytona, FL

I once did some shows in a place called **Daytona**, which is in Florida. Which is in the United States of America. Which is just south of Canada.

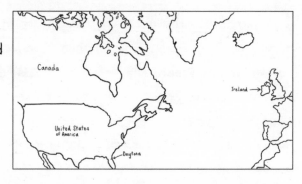

Which is just the other side of Ireland. I talked about sharks during my show and, afterwards, a man called Hank, or Franklin J. Plankton Junior or something, told me that Daytona is not only a shark attack hotspot but is also one of the places in the world where you are most likely to get **struck by lightning**.

So if you live in Daytona, Florida, you are quite likely to be struck by lightning AND bitten by a shark. I wonder if anyone has had both things happen to them on the same day! Or maybe someone was being attacked by a shark, then the shark got hit by lightning! That would be handy. Or maybe someone got hit by lightning and was then rescued by a shark.

Where is your imagination?

I bet people are always telling you to use your **imagination**.

But where is it?

Do we each have our own separate imagination, or is there like a massive imaginary land called Imagination which is looked after by space whales and Airedale terriers? When we think of ideas, are we just downloading them from this place?

Is your imagination somewhere inside your brain? Or is your brain somewhere inside your imagination?

Imagine if you didn't have a brain at all. You were actually just imagining it.

What are you imagining it with?

I can't find my swimming costume.

IMAGINATION LAND

Just use your imagination.

Toffee fudge dolphin: Page 216

Blender shark: Page 201

Lemon meringue pie shark: Page 221

Making up things just to sound funny: Page 182

Different types of teeth

If you have a look around in your mouth you will notice that your teeth are not all the same shape and size. Some are pointy, some are flat, some have holes in them, some are gold and some are black. Well that's what mine are like, anyway.

It's the same with sharks.

There are **four basic types of shark teeth** and they all have different purposes.

DENSE, FLAT TEETH are used for **crushing** things like crabs and mussels.

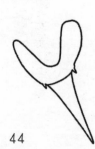

NEEDLE-LIKE TEETH are used for catching **small prey**, like fish, squid and stingrays.

TRIANGULAR TEETH are for catching **big prey**, like seals, dolphins and other sharks. These teeth have jagged edges, like steak knives.

NON-FUNCTIONAL TEETH are found in sharks like basking sharks and whale sharks, sharks that don't do any biting any more but just live on **plankton**. These teeth are a sort of evolutionary unnecessary bit of a shark. A bit like men's nipples.

My nan also had four sets of **false teeth**. Each one was for a different occasion. She had talking teeth, eating teeth, singing teeth and teeth for hunting fish and turtles.

Shark teeth:
Page 28

Anatomy
of a shark:
Page 69

Different types
of shark attack:
Page 184

The lightning channel

What seals should really do is watch TV programmes about being struck by lightning. Then the statistics would be in their favour. It would start off with lots of footage of really scary lightning and then the voiceover would say:

'Welcome to Seal TV. Lightning is really scary. But you are more likely to be attacked by a shark than you are to be struck by lightning. Unless you are a TREE!'

But if a baby tree saw that programme, they might be **really scared**.

TV shows for seals: Page 38

Daytona, FL: Page 42

Don't worry!

So, basically, sharks are nothing to worry about unless you are a seal, or another sort of animal that sharks like to eat. Like a dolphin or a crab or a banana or a stingray or another shark.

Obviously, there are lots of different types of shark that all like to eat different things. So I've made a handy and unnecessarily complicated table, which is on page 142.

Different sharks/ different food: Page 142

It would be very helpful if you wanted to keep a pet shark. There would be no point buying a fine pair of hammerhead sharks from your local pet shop and then trying to feed them granola!

Hammerhead shark: Page 59

In **The Funny Life of Pets**, there is a story about a lady called Barbara who keeps tiger sharks in her bathroom in Devon. I'm not sure what she feeds them, though.

Can you keep pet sharks?: Page 150

Sharks are really old

How many sharks get eaten by people?: Page 55

Trying to understand really big numbers: Page 194

What sharks are like when they are old: Page 198

The oldest shark: Page 199

Sharks have been with us for about 450 million years. We know this because it says so in a vlog recorded in 449,999,800 BCE by the prehistoric YouTuber DINO245, who filmed himself standing on a beach talking about his shoes, and then saw a shark fin in the water behind him.

Whoa! I've never seen one of those before!

Weirdly, some old people are about 450 million years old. They are still alive but live in maximum-security homes. They don't have watchtowers or anything. Just loads of stairs on the way out.

Lemon shark

These sharks are a sort of yellowy colour, which is why they are called lemon sharks. If I was in charge of naming sharks I would have called them **'dusty custard sharks'**.

Lemon sharks give birth to live young and do so in nursery areas in mangrove forests on coasts. This gives their babies somewhere safe to live until they are big enough to go out into the ocean on their own.

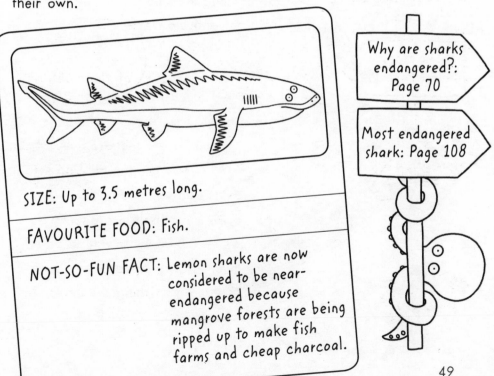

SIZE: Up to 3.5 metres long.

FAVOURITE FOOD: Fish.

NOT-SO-FUN FACT: Lemon sharks are now considered to be near-endangered because mangrove forests are being ripped up to make fish farms and cheap charcoal.

Why are sharks endangered?: Page 70

Most endangered shark: Page 108

Kuala Lumpur

I was once in a bar in **Malaysia**. Which is just the other side of Thailand. On the way to Mablethorpe.

As I was sitting enjoying a nice glass of cola, I looked up and saw a set of square fish tanks running along the ceiling. Inside these tanks were a dozen **baby tiger sharks**, just swimming around looking cool. I asked the barman what they did when the sharks grew too big, and he said that when that happened they just pulled them out and ate them!

This was the first time I had ever heard of anyone eating a shark. I didn't even know that you could eat sharks. It must take quite a while to get the wrapper off! This got me thinking — how many people get eaten by sharks? And how many sharks get eaten by people?

MENU
COLA
BANANAS
TIGER SHARK

A menu of endangered species: Page 68

Oakley's mum: Page 79

How many people get eaten by sharks?

OK. So. I've done some proper research on this and over the last 50 years, on average, the number of people in the whole world who get **eaten by sharks** every year is ... on the next page ... Are you ready ...?

Five or,

at most, six.

That's it. **Five or six** people get eaten by a shark each year. In the whole world.

Now, obviously, if you are one of those five or six people, that's **horrible** and I'm really sorry that happened to you.

But let's compare that to how many sharks get eaten by people ...

How much do sharks eat?: Page 100

Sharks do not think we are tasty: Page 113

Things that are more likely to kill you than sharks: Page 160

How many sharks get eaten by people?

Again, I've done some proper research here, and it's quite hard to get an exact figure because when someone gets eaten by a shark, it gets on the news everywhere. But when someone eats a shark, **no one really cares**.

And in other news, Mr Perkins from Kent just ate a tin of tuna.

But the general estimate is that the number of sharks that **WE eat** each and every year is currently about ...

One Hundred Million!

That's **100,000,000 sharks** that get eaten by people across the world every year.

That's **274,000 sharks** every day.

Trying to understand really big numbers: Page 194

That's three sharks **every second**.

In the time it took you to read this page, about 200 sharks got eaten by **human beings**.

One hundred million is a very big number. Most people find it really hard to imagine a really big number.

So it would seem that rather than humans being afraid of sharks, sharks should be afraid of humans!

Who is eating all these sharks and why?: Page 62

Shark finning: Page 64

Oakley's mum: Page 79

Hammerhead shark

These are possibly the **funniest-looking** sharks. Their heads are literally shaped like a hammer. We still don't know exactly why they have evolved to be like this. Some people think that by having a really wide head, their eyes and special sensors, called 'ampullae of Lorenzini', are further apart, which means they are better at finding prey.

Anatomy of a shark: Page 69

In the daytime, they hang around in schools of other hammerheads, just swimming about and chatting to their mates. But then at night-time, they swim down and cruise the ocean floor looking for food.

To me, they look a bit like vacuum cleaners when they are doing this.

How big are sharks?: Page 60

Famous types of shark: Page 18

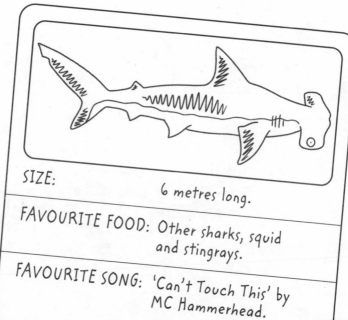

SIZE: 6 metres long.

FAVOURITE FOOD: Other sharks, squid and stingrays.

FAVOURITE SONG: 'Can't Touch This' by MC Hammerhead.

How big are sharks?

The **smallest** shark in the world is the dwarf lantern shark, which is only 14 centimetres long. The longest is the whale shark, which grows up to 10 metres, or 41½ feet. It doesn't have 41½ feet. What you're thinking of there is approximately half a centipede. That's a completely different thing.

I don't want to be in this book.

Here is a handy illustration that compares the size of different sharks:

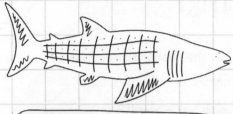

Whale shark – 12.5 metres

Whale shark: Page 86

London bus – 12.2 metres

Great white shark – 6 metres

Great white shark: Page 21

Hammerhead shark – 6 metres

Hammerhead shark: Page 59

African elephant – 3.3 metres

Lemon shark – 3.4 metres

Lemon shark: Page 49

Wobbegong – 1.2 metres

Dwarf lantern shark – 15 centimetres

Who is eating all these sharks and why?

You probably don't see shark on the menu of your local restaurant or takeaway establishment.

But in many parts of the world, it is perfectly possible to buy shark steaks at a fishmonger's, take them home and cook them for your dinner.

I choose **not** to eat shark. I'm sort of allergic to lots of different fish and I don't know if I'm allergic to shark or not. But, anyway, it seems to me that we've done a lot to damage the ocean and as a part of what I can do to help the climate change emergency, I think it's probably best to stop taking things out of the ocean for a while and let it **recover** from humans.

But I understand that shark steak is a really **nutritious** and healthy food.

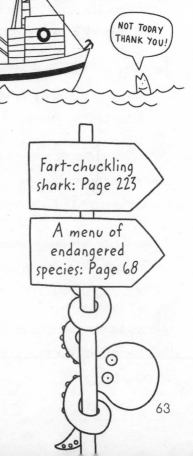

NOT TODAY THANK YOU!

The thing is though, that most of the 100,000,000 sharks that are killed each year are not turned into shark steaks. Most of them are **finned**.

Fart-chuckling shark: Page 223

A menu of endangered species: Page 68

Until I started writing this book I had never heard of finning. I find the whole thing really **disturbing**. If you don't want to read about it, don't read the next page. Just skip it and find something funny.

Shark finning

Many years ago, someone invented a recipe for something called **'shark fin soup'**.

In parts of Asia and other parts of the world, shark fin soup became a really **expensive** meal to order in a restaurant. It was basically a way of showing off to all your friends.

Similarly, lots of people eat **caviar** to show how fancy they are, even though caviar is disgusting. They don't like the taste but everyone gets really impressed when they eat it.

Shark fins are very expensive for restaurants to buy at a fishmonger. And this means that fisherfolk get paid a lot of money for bringing in shark fins from their boats.

Because lots of sharks are **threatened** as a species, there is a limit on the amount of shark that fisherfolk are allowed to catch.

In most countries, however, this amount is based on the **weight** of shark meat that is brought into the harbour, not the number of sharks that have been killed.

So this means that what lots of fisherfolk do when they catch a shark is cut its fin off with a knife, keep the fin, and then throw the rest of the shark back into the sea, where it bleeds to death and gets eaten by other sharks.

The very thought of this makes me really, **really angry.**

But lots of people have been doing a great deal of good to help sort this problem out.

What you can do to help endangered species: Page 224

Things that should not be in this book: Page 236

Yao Ming

Yao Ming is a basketball player from China. I've never met him, but from pictures he looks like he's about as tall as a giraffe and twice as cool. Yao played for the Shanghai Sharks, which is an excellent name for a basketball team. Because of this, Yao Ming became interested in sharks.

One day he found out about shark finning and was so **horrified** by the whole thing that he started campaigning to **protect** sharks and stop people from eating shark fin soup.

He made a TV advert where he's sitting in a fancy restaurant. Everyone around him is eating shark fin soup. Then he looks over at a fish tank in the wall. Inside it a finned shark is bleeding to death and Yao Ming pushes his dish of soup away in disgust. Then everyone else does the same thing.

It's a really powerful advert, and Yao Ming is very famous and influential in China and in the world. And he's used his influence to do something good! Because of his advert, the lives of around 50 million sharks have been **saved**.

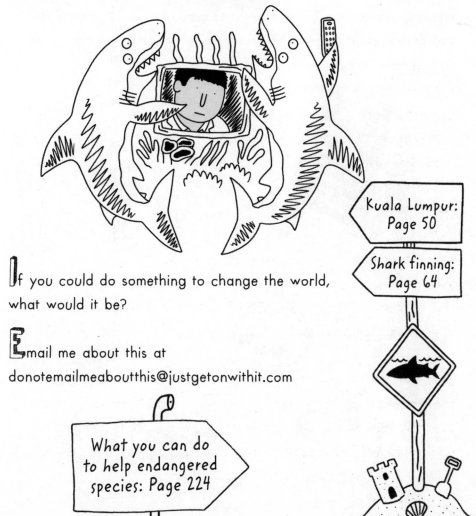

If you could do something to change the world, what would it be?

Email me about this at donotemailmeaboutthis@justgetonwithit.com

Kuala Lumpur: Page 50

Shark finning: Page 64

What you can do to help endangered species: Page 224

A menu of endangered species

Taking an endangered species and making a fancy sort of dish out of it is pretty weird. So, welcome to my new restaurant, The Deep-Fried Dodo!

Skylark sandwiches

Today's Specials
Skylark Sandwiches
Tiger Sausages
Rhinoceros Burgers
Orangutan Ice-Cream
Shark Fin Soup

Tiger sausages

Orang-utan ice cream

Rhinoceros burgers

Shark Fin soup

Things we don't love and wouldn't save if they were endangered: Page 172

Anatomy of a shark

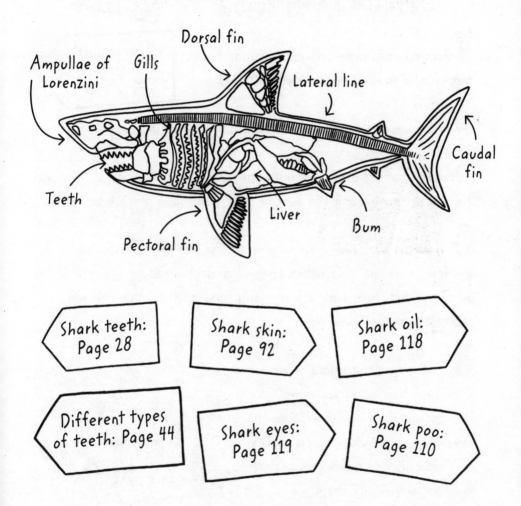

Ampullae of Lorenzini

Gills

Dorsal fin

Lateral line

Teeth

Pectoral fin

Liver

Bum

Caudal fin

Shark teeth: Page 28

Shark skin: Page 92

Shark oil: Page 118

Different types of teeth: Page 44

Shark eyes: Page 119

Shark poo: Page 110

Why are sharks endangered?

Most endangered shark: Page 108

Survival of the fittest: Page 140

There is really only one reason that sharks are endangered: **humans**.

Sharks were doing absolutely fine until we came along.

Sharks are in trouble because they have babies quite slowly and they have to be quite old before they can make more baby sharks.

All animals can evolve to survive things like changes in the weather, movement of other species and changes to the landscape, but these naturally take a very long time and animals are able to **adapt** at the same rate.

But all animals struggle when we mess with their habitat in some way. The changes we are making to the environment are happening so fast that animals don't have enough time to change the way they live.

NOT-SO-CAMOUFLAGED HARES

The Cairngorms are a group of mountains in
Scotland, and are home to the mountain hare.
In the summertime it is brown, and blends
in with the heather and grass. In the
wintertime, its coat changes to white so that
it is **camouflaged** in the snow.

Because of climate change, snow in the
Cairngorms is coming later and later each year. But the mountain
hare is still turning white at the same time it always used to. This
means that during early winter, the mountains are still green and
brown and the hare is white. Now the hare is really easily spotted
by eagles and other birds of prey who can see them a mile away.
If things carry on the way they are, mountain
hares will be **extinct** in the Cairngorms
within a few years.

What you can do
to help endangered
species: Page 224

BABY SHARK BARBECUE

In the oceans, if we change the **temperature** of the water or remove parts of it, it changes the whole ocean and sea creatures struggle. Lemon sharks, for example, give birth in **mangrove swamps**. These are important nurseries for baby sharks because other sharks that would eat them in the open ocean can't swim into the mangroves.

But humans are destroying mangrove trees very quickly. At least one-third of all the mangroves in the world have been **destroyed** already. Usually it's because areas are being cleared to turn into fish farms or harbours. Often the mangrove trees themselves are turned into cheap barbecue charcoal.

Lemon shark:
Page 49

Something that
hunts great whites:
Page 174

If there's nowhere for baby sharks, then it won't be long before there aren't any adult sharks either.

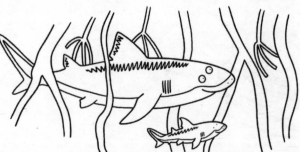

72

If you don't like the sound of all this, don't buy your barbecue charcoal from a supermarket. Get locally **coppiced charcoal**. It makes the food taste nicer too!

Most sharks are 'apex predators' and they have a very important part to play in the ecosystem. Apex predators are at the **top** of the food chain. If there are no sharks, then the things that sharks eat will have no predators. This means their population will get out of control, and they'll eat all of their prey until there are none of those animals left.

Sharks are not just beautiful (and quite scary-looking) animals. They are hugely **important** to the world.

How sharks do good in the ocean: Page 154

Why aren't there any dangerous animals in the UK?: Page 136

The Wolves of Yellowstone

Lots of people think that apex predators should be **reintroduced** to areas of wilderness, and this is what happened in Yellowstone National Park in the USA.

Yellowstone isn't a park like the one at the bottom of your road, with a couple of swings and a slide. It is over 100 kilometres long and 80 kilometres wide.

Before people turned up, there were loads of wolves in Yellowstone. But by the 20th century, they had been hunted to **extinction**. Because of this, the elk had no predators and their population got really big, really quickly. Elk eat baby trees, so after a while there were hardly any trees left. And nearly all wildlife disappeared from the park ...

The Airedale Air Museum: Page 102

Fish friends: Page 116

WOLVES MEET YELLOWSTONE

In 1995, wolves were reintroduced to Yellowstone as a way to **control** the elk population.

It turns out that they did so much more than that. They re-engineered the whole ecosystem.

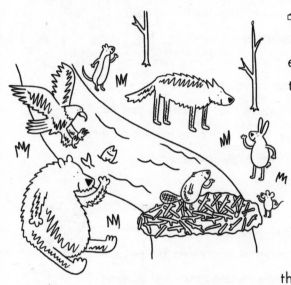

The wolves did eat a few elk, but more importantly, they changed the elks' behaviour. The elk began avoiding places where they could be ambushed and trapped, places like gorges and river banks. This allowed more trees to grow beside rivers, and then different birds and fish turned up, and beavers came back. Beavers build dams in rivers to slow down the flow so they have a better place to live. And the dams created more habitats for other creatures that hadn't been seen in Yellowstone for years. All because of the wolves.

Survival of the fittest: Page 140

CABBAGES!

I did something similar in my vegetable garden. I got really annoyed by pigeons eating my cabbages so I bought a pair of **golden eagles** and made them a home by nailing an old Wendy house to the top of the shed. The eagles got rid of the pigeons, but that wasn't the only thing that happened.

First of all, my children were afraid to go in the garden in case they were pecked on the head by an eagle. This meant they spent more time running around inside the house and quickly wore out the carpets.

When we pulled up the old carpets, we discovered a trapdoor in the floorboards, and after opening it up we found a portal to another world ruled by clock bears. These are small chocolate-coloured bears with extremely complex clocks inside their tummies.

We're not sure what their purpose is yet, but I think they might control space and time.

Where is your imagination?: Page 43

Making things up just to sound funny: Page 182

REEF ECOSYSTEMS

If wolves can affect the whole landscape of Yellowstone Park, then what are sharks doing to their own ecosystem? It's quite easy to see what's going on in Yellowstone, but the oceans are a lot more murky. So far, human beings have only explored about 5% of the oceans, so we don't really know what's

going on down there. But just take a look at **blacktip reef sharks**, which spend lots of time swimming around coral reefs eating fish. If we kill all the blacktips, there will be nothing to eat all the fish. The population of fish will increase really quickly, and they will eat all the coral. Coral is a really

important habitat; it protects coastlines from erosion and absorbs carbon from the atmosphere: carbon that changes our climate.

Sharks are a hugely **important** part of the world.

We need to look after them.

How sharks do good in the oceans: Page 154

Hawaii sharks: Page 178

Blacktip reef shark: Page 167

Do sharks sleep?

Most sharks must have water continually flowing over their gills to breathe, so they can never sleep. Maybe that's why they look so grumpy. They just want to rest their eyes.

Imagine if you had to be always walking around because otherwise you'd stop breathing? You'd get quite annoyed after a while.

Zebra sharks are one of the few sharks that can stay still without drowning. They do this using something called 'buccal pumping'. This means that they use the muscles in their mouth to suck water in and spit it towards their gills.

Why grown-ups rest their eyes: Page 166

Moving forwards: Page 40

Oakley's Mum

The other day I was visiting a primary school in Suffolk and I got talking about sharks. A boy there called Oakley said that his mum had caught, cooked and eaten a shark. Now, obviously, what Oakley's mum does is her business, I'm sure she's a lovely person and at least she ate the whole shark rather than just the fin, but I wonder if somewhere sharks are queueing up to go to the shark cinema to watch a horror movie called:

OAKLEY'S MUM!

She catches you. She cooks you. She eats you.

Jaws: Page 34

Jersey Shore Cow Massacre!: Page 215

Who is eating all these sharks and why?: Page 62

How many sharks get eaten by people?: Page 55

How do sharks navigate?

If you're in the car and you want to get somewhere, you can put the destination into your **satnav**.

Sharks, however, have an amazing ability to navigate through the dark, murky waters of the oceans all by themselves. **Tiger sharks** can follow exactly the same route each day through featureless miles of blue. Some sharks even swim across entire oceans to get to breeding or feeding grounds.

So how do they do it without getting lost and having to ask a turtle for directions?

Excuse me. Could you tell me the way to the mangrove swamps?

Yes. You go in that direction and just keep swimming ... away from me.

Well, no one is exactly sure, because it's very difficult to know what's going on in a shark's brain.

Some research suggests that sharks use the Earth's **magnetic field** to work out where they are.

Sharks have some extremely sensitive **sensors** in their nose called the 'ampullae of Lorenzini'. These can detect the tiniest changes in water temperature. Zoologists reckon that sharks use these to navigate.

And also, older sharks might simply just remember where everything is. A bit like my father-in-law Colin. He spent lots of years as a delivery driver and so he knows the name and number of pretty much every road in East Anglia, where all the service stations are, the names of all the people who worked in those service stations, and the exact locations of every near-accident he ever had.

Hammerhead shark: Page 59

How many seas are there?: Page 146

Tiger shark: Page 33

Moving forwards: Page 40

My phobia of sharks

So, how did I become afraid of sharks? Well, it probably started when I watched **Jaws**. That was enough to make me start thinking about sharks that eat people.

But because I was brought up in the UK, I never really had to worry about sharks. Generally speaking, if you stay out of the water, you don't have to worry about sharks at all. If you're walking down the high street of your local town, the chances of being attacked by a shark are very, very slim.

If sharks learn to ride scooters, however, then we will all be in a lot of trouble.

Jaws:
Page 34

Why aren't there any dangerous animals in the UK?:
Page 136

Lots of people are afraid of all sorts of things. These things may include small spaces, open spaces, spiders, dogs, heights, sandwiches and your mum. My sister-in-law is afraid of Shirley Bassey.

Things we are afraid of and why: Page 152

Who the crumbling plimpturtle is Shirley Bassey?: Page 192

Some **phobias** are really hard to manage because the thing people are afraid of is all over the place. If you're afraid of cats, you might struggle to leave the house.

If you happen to be afraid of spiders, you have quite a problem. Spiders can be anywhere ... You could wake up in the morning to find a spider dangling from the ceiling over your face! And you would yell, 'Flumbling snot-trousers! Mum! There's a spider in my room! Help!'

Irrational fear of sharks: Page 98

Primal fear: Page 202

83

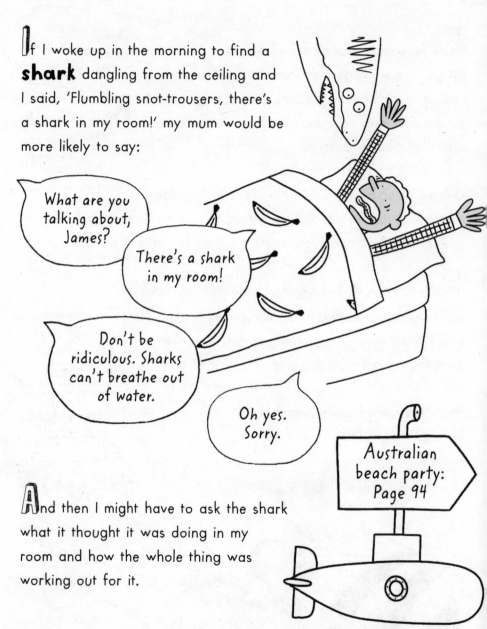

If I woke up in the morning to find a **shark** dangling from the ceiling and I said, 'Flumbling snot-trousers, there's a shark in my room!' my mum would be more likely to say:

What are you talking about, James?

There's a shark in my room!

Don't be ridiculous. Sharks can't breathe out of water.

Oh yes. Sorry.

Australian beach party: Page 94

And then I might have to ask the shark what it thought it was doing in my room and how the whole thing was working out for it.

The conversation might go something like this:

ME: Hello.

SHARK: Hello yourself.

ME: Are you a shark?

SHARK: Yes. Tiger shark. You?

ME: No. Human.

SHARK: Can I help you?

ME: Yes. I was just wondering if you can breathe out of the water?

SHARK: No. I can't.

ME: And have you tried breathing recently?

SHARK: No. Let me give it a go. Oh no. I can't breathe. I'm dying. Eurrgghhhh.

ME: That serves you right for being on my ceiling, doesn't it?

And if it did die, then the shark might land on your head. Which would be really annoying.

A dead shark landing on your head: Page 89

How I got over my phobia of sharks: Page 104

Whale shark

This is not only the biggest shark in the world. It's the biggest fish of any kind.

It can grow up to **10 metres** long!

They are called whale sharks because they are as big as a whale, but they are not actually whales.

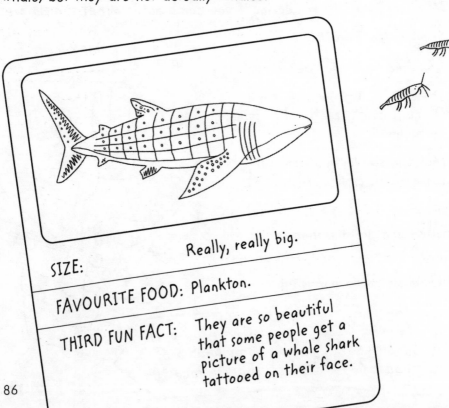

SIZE: Really, really big.

FAVOURITE FOOD: Plankton.

THIRD FUN FACT: They are so beautiful that some people get a picture of a whale shark tattooed on their face.

Whale sharks are **filter-feeders**, which means they swim around with their mouth open and filter out bits of **krill**, very tiny shrimp-like creatures, which become their dinner. My nan does a similar thing with gravy.

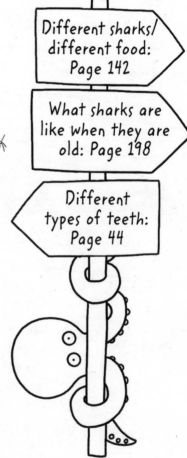

Different sharks/ different food: Page 142

What sharks are like when they are old: Page 198

Different types of teeth: Page 44

Whale sharks live for a very long time – some scientists reckon they live for up to **130 years!** I bet they'd have some great stories to tell. Although most of those stories would probably be about eating krill, I suppose.

Wobbegong

Wobbegong means **'shaggy beard'** in one of the many Aboriginal languages of Australia.

They're also known as **'carpet sharks'** because they look like a bit of shaggy carpet and are bottom-dwellers.

This doesn't mean that they live in your bottom. No one wants a shark living in their bottom.

Wobbegongs hang around in shallow waters and they are ambush predators, staying perfectly still until their prey wanders past. Then they move with lightning speed and swallow their prey whole.

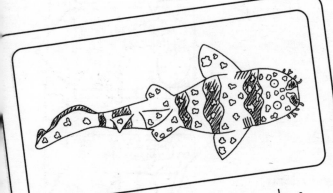

SIZE: About 2 metres long.

FAVOURITE FOOD: Fish, although they do have a habit of biting people's feet if they get trodden on.

EXTRA FUN FACT: If you wear a wobbegong as a hat, you instantly look like Donald Trump.

A dead shark landing on your head

Imagine a dead shark landing on your head. Would that kill you?

It probably would.

Imagine being killed by having a shark landing on your head. How embarrassing would that be?

My phobia of sharks: Page 82

Things that are more likely to kill you than sharks: Page 160

Extreme coconuts: Page 200

Would a shark kill you if it landed on your head?

Obviously, I like to be as **factually accurate** as I can. So we need to know, would a shark kill you if it fell from the ceiling and landed on your head?

So I phoned my godson, David, who has a degree in Physics from the Oxford University of Cleverness and is currently in charge of a nuclear power station.

According to science, the two **variables** in a 'shark-falling-on-head' experiment are the weight of the shark and the height of the ceiling. Variables are things in experiments that, when they're changed, change the result of the experiment too. So, the heavier the shark, the more likely the fall is to be fatal. And the higher the ceiling, the faster the shark will be travelling when it hits you, so it's more likely to squash your head.

You need to calculate the **weight** of the shark and the **height** of the ceiling. If that puts you below the curved line on the graph below, you are safe from death by falling shark. Anything above the line and you're in **a lot of danger** indeed.

According to David, 'The line is curved because the chance of death from shark drop is due to shark momentum (mass proportional to momentum, height proportional to momentum squared). Doubling the height the shark falls from is as dangerous as quadrupling the weight of the shark.'

So if you live in a hobbit house with low ceilings you could probably cope with something as big as a hammerhead shark landing on your head. BUT if you're lucky enough to live in a house with really high ceilings, any shark bigger than a lemon shark would probably cause you to shuffle off this mortal coil.

A dead shark landing on your head: Page 89

Things that are more likely to kill you than sharks: Page 160

Shark skin

Sharks have **very thick** skin. It can be up to 10 centimetres thick. This means that you can make all sorts of jokes about sharks and they don't mind at all.

Jokes about sharks: Page 210

So, a shark's skin is about 25 times thicker than the skin on the bottom of your foot!

People always say that sharks' teeth are really scary-looking. But their skin is pretty dangerous. It's made of sharp, triangular scales that are more like teeth than the sort of scales you'd find on normal fish.

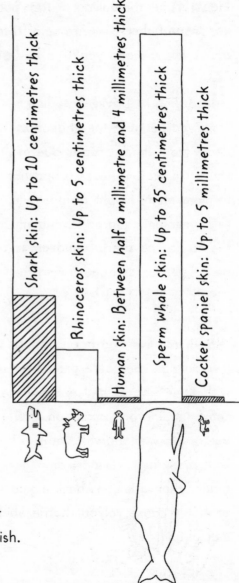

Shark skin: Up to 10 centimetres thick

Rhinoceros skin: Up to 5 centimetres thick

Human skin: Between half a millimetre and 4 millimetres thick

Sperm whale skin: Up to 35 centimetres thick

Cocker spaniel skin: Up to 5 millimetres thick

So basically, that's an animal with loads of teeth, wearing **a suit of armour** that's made out of teeth.

That's like a hedgehog covered in stinging nettles!

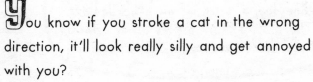

Or a lion covered in angry badgers.

Shark teeth: Page 28

Or a farty supply teacher covered in tiny, farty supply teachers.

You know if you stroke a cat in the wrong direction, it'll look really silly and get annoyed with you?

Well, if you stroke a shark in ANY direction, your hands will turn into Parmesan cheese!

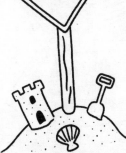

Australian beach party

My phobia of sharks really kicked off when I was visiting Australia. Where I live in the UK, you see, there are literally no dangerous sharks at all. There aren't really any dangerous anythings.

Why aren't there any dangerous animals in the UK?: Page 136

But in Australia, there are all sorts of dangerous animals. And sharks are one of them.

I now know that the chances of being eaten by a shark are extremely small, but at the time I had no idea. In my head, people were getting bitten by sharks every day.

On Monday, I got bitten by a shark — took my arm clean off. On Tuesday, a shark bit my leg off. On Wednesday, a shark bit my other leg off. On Thursday, a shark bit my other arm off. And I don't want to talk about Friday.

I was in Australia for the Adelaide Fringe Festival.

Where is Adelaide?: Page 112

One night there was a birthday party for someone called John, who was from the UK too. In fact, everyone else at the party was from the UK. We had a barbecue on the beach and some of us had a little paddle in the ocean as the sun set. It was lovely. **BUT!!!**

The next morning, I told the barista about the party the night before. He was Australian, and when I told him we had gone paddling in the sea at dusk, he told me that we were snot-trousering **maroonatics!**

How many people get eaten by sharks?: Page 51

My phobia of sharks: Page 82

How many seas are there?: Page 146

It turns out that no one sensible goes into the ocean **at dusk** because that is when sharks come close to the shore to feed!

And then, even though nothing terrible had happened, I began to imagine great white sharks circling around us!

That night I had **a nightmare** and, after that, I refused to go anywhere near the ocean in Australia.

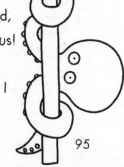

95

Sharks in New Zealand

One of the **best things** about New Zealand is that there are no dangerous sharks in the waters there. One day when I was visiting that lovely country, I went swimming with some friends in the ocean. As I was floating around, I **felt something** bump into my leg. Now, it might just have been a piece of seaweed or one of my friends kicking me. But in my mind, it was a **deadly shark**, checking me out to see if I was edible.

It was at that moment that I realised just how fast I could swim!

I swam so fast there was fire coming out the top of my head!

I was so frightened that I farted continuously – like a jet engine.

The jet-farting probably made me travel even faster.

In fact, when I got to the beach and was out of the water, I carried on swimming anyway.

I swam into the sand.

I swam into the ground.

I swam towards the centre of the Earth.

Irrational fear of sharks!: Page 98

Primal fear: Page 202

People gathered around me as I dug myself a hole like a super-turtle.

Now, I'm sure that what bumped into me wasn't really a shark, of course, BUT after that day I realised that I had become utterly **terrified** of sharks. I had a phobia. A phobia of sharks!

Retrieving bricks from the bottom of the pool in your pyjamas: Page 186

Irrational fear of sharks

My incidents of paddling in the ocean in Adelaide and being bumped by something in New Zealand had kicked off some sort of **primal fear** in my brain and I had become terrified of sharks.

At the time I thought it was actually quite normal to be afraid of a man-eating monster because I didn't realise that sharks very, very **rarely** attack people.

But, in my head, I was in **danger**. I wouldn't go in the ocean anywhere in the world where sharks might live. I went to Florida and refused to go in the ocean. I went to Australia again and said no to getting my feet wet. I went to Malaysia and wouldn't even look at the Indian Ocean.

It got **so bad** that I started refusing to go in the sea at home where there is literally no danger of sharks at all.

Primal fear:
Page 202

I wouldn't go in the sea at Hunstanton, Brighton or Devon. Anywhere! **Just in case** there was a shark.

I didn't even like going to indoor swimming pools because every time I went near the water, the **Jaws** music started playing in my head and I had to run back into the changing rooms where it was safe. (Even though more people are injured from slipping over in swimming-pool changing rooms than are attacked by sharks.)

Things that are more likely to kill you than sharks: Page 160

How much do sharks eat?

Different sharks/different food: Page 142

Great white shark: Page 21

It really depends on the size and type of the shark.

Great white sharks need to eat about 11 tonnes of food a year. That's about the same as eating **350,000 burgers**.

They can, however, go for up to **three months** without eating anything at all.

If you compare that to other animals, rabbits eat fairly constantly, whereas lions only need to eat about once a week.

Eleven-year-old boys and girls on the other hand have to eat something sugary or salty every seven minutes or they implode and leak all over the furniture.

Would you like a hot dog?

No thanks, I had a sandwich in February.

Sharks do not think we are tasty: Page 113

Bull shark

Bull sharks are famously **aggressive**. They don't like the taste of people but they will often attack people if they are in their territory.

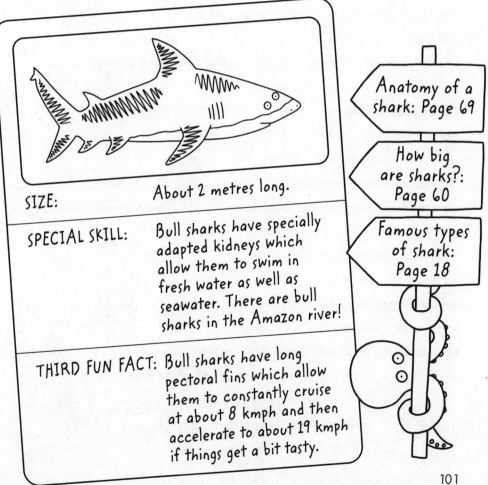

SIZE: About 2 metres long.

SPECIAL SKILL: Bull sharks have specially adapted kidneys which allow them to swim in fresh water as well as seawater. There are bull sharks in the Amazon river!

THIRD FUN FACT: Bull sharks have long pectoral fins which allow them to constantly cruise at about 8 kmph and then accelerate to about 19 kmph if things get a bit tasty.

Anatomy of a shark: Page 69

How big are sharks?: Page 60

Famous types of shark: Page 18

The Airedale Air Museum

My favourite museum in the whole world is the Airedale Air Museum in Airedale, West Yorkshire. Most air museums contain aeroplanes and helicopters. The Airedale Air Museum, however, is a museum of **air**.

Thousands upon thousands of bottles and containers of air. It's absolutely **fascinating**.

There is a room that contains the last breaths of many famous people. I particularly like the last breath of Mary, Queen of Scots. That must have been pretty tricky to catch.

Another room contains the farts of various famous people who have donated their stinky bottom burps to the museum for posterity. On one shelf is a whole **row of farts** of movie stars and musicians. There you can see the bottled farts of Judi Dench, Justin Timberlake and Adele.

In the future we might be able to bring various famous people back from the dead by using **DNA** from the farts curated by the Airedale Air Museum.

The museum is quite hard to find. They did have a giant wooden fart sign on the roof but one day it **blew off**.

Where is your imagination?:
Page 43

My best friend is a shark:
Page 126

Frugal Sharkish:
Page 169

In the 1980s, the sharkily named **Frugal Sharkish** worked at the Airedale Air Museum.

How I got over my phobia of sharks

I now don't have a phobia of sharks. It only lasted for about five or six years. But how did I **get over it?**

My phobia of sharks: Page 82

Well, I learned from listening to all sorts of people that the way to get over a fear is to **face it**.

I needed to find out more about sharks: Page 26

At first, this didn't make any sense at all. Surely if you're afraid of something, you should **run away** from it because it is dangerous!

But apparently the best way to deal with things you are afraid of IS to go right up to them and look them in the eye. It's quite hard to do this with sharks. But for me, the fear had become actually **getting in water.**

One day I was invited back to Australia to do a show at the Perth Literary Festival. All the British writers were treated to a boat trip, where we could all jump off the boat and swim around a reef looking at fish and stuff. That idea, of course, filled me with absolute **dread** and **fear**.

The other writers on the boat were much more famous than me. So famous that I have had to change their names for legal reasons. Along with the others, there was Scarlett Feverington, who writes spy novels and used to be **AN ACTUAL SPY**, like James Bond.

I reckoned that if there were any problems with sharks around the reef, Scarlett Feverington would know what to do. She probably had lasers in her flippers. Lasers that could slice a shark in two if it came near me. My plan was to stick close to Scarlett and if a shark turned up, get behind her.

Australian beach party: Page 94

Very quickly, though, everyone disappeared into the water, leaving me on my own, staring into the Indian Ocean, wondering what murderous fish were down there waiting for me. There was **NO WAY** I was getting in there.

But then I looked across to the shore and saw the most beautiful beach, about 100 metres away. **Something** in my head told me that if I could jump off and swim to the beach, it would be a good thing. I didn't have to go snorkelling. I could just jump off and swim over there. So I did. (Well, I didn't jump. I sort of dangled limply from a ladder crying for about five minutes, and then dropped awkwardly into the ocean like a difficult poo.)

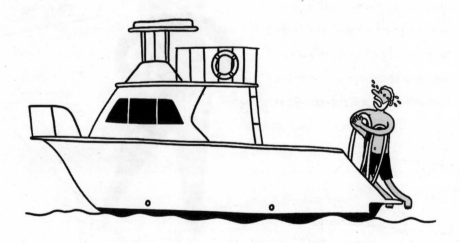

It felt like it took **forever** to swim to the beach. Eventually, exhausted, I made it and lay on the sand, like a shipwreck survivor, thanking all the powers in the universe that had kept me safe.

I was a little bit shaky when I got back to the boat but I spent the rest of the day beaming from ear to ear. What I had done was nothing big to any of the people around me, or probably to most people in the world. But for me, I had done something **extraordinary!**

Something worse than sharks: Page 196

Swimming with sharks: Page 232

How to overcome fear: Page 230

107

Most endangered shark

The most endangered shark in the world is the **blue shark**. This is because people kill them for their skins, because they are blue. Apparently, having a pair of shoes made from blue shark skin is really cool-looking.

The moral of this story is: **Don't be blue**. It just attracts unwanted attention.

The other moral of this story is: If you are going to be blue, try and avoid people who will turn you into a **leather jacket** ...

DRY CLEAN ONLY

Nice ink, mate.

Why are sharks endangered?: Page 70

Shark skin: Page 92

What you can do to help endangered species: Page 224

Thresher shark

This fascinating shark has a tail that is almost as long as its body. It's basically a tail with a mouth at one end.

The thresher shark attacks schools of fish by rounding them up and then whipping them with its tail. This stuns or kills the fish, making it very easy for the thresher shark to turn around and gobble all the fish up.

Anatomy of a shark: Page 69

This is exactly the same way that my mother-in-law does **babysitting**.

How to defend yourself against a shark attack: Page 188

Sometimes thresher sharks use their tails to whip a tub of cream into a pavlova, but it isn't very nice because it's hard to get hold of fresh raspberries when you live in the sea – and don't have any thumbs.

SIZE: Up to 6 metres long.

FAVOURITE FOOD: Fish.

Shark poo

If you have **pet fish** in a tank, you'll know that they tend to poo while swimming along. Sometimes the poo hangs out of their bottom for **ages!**

So as sharks are a type of fish, do they do something similar?

Well, I've done lots of research about this, and it seems that sharks tend to shoot their poo out of their bum, a bit like a **liquid bottom burp**.

I found an article on the internet about a zoologist called Alistair Dove, who photographed a whale shark doing a poo and got very excited about this. 'It could be a literal gold mine,' he said.

I think what he means is that if we are able to **study shark poo**, it will tell us some really interesting things.

Shark poo is an important part of the **ecosystem**. It contains all sorts of nutrients that smaller fish can eat, and is a kind of **fertiliser** for the ocean floor. In the same way that we put horse poo on our vegetable gardens, sharks poo on the gardens of the sea.

If you look on YouTube, you'll also find a very funny video of a great white shark doing a poo on a load of **scuba divers**.

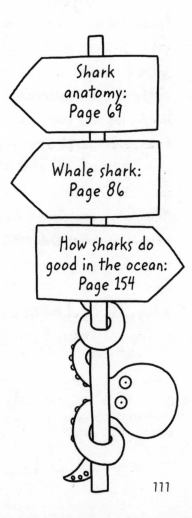

Shark anatomy: Page 69

Whale shark: Page 86

How sharks do good in the ocean: Page 154

Where is Adelaide?

Adelaide is on the south coast of Australia.

Look. Here it is on a map.

You'll notice that it is on the Great Australian Bight. This is a body of water that contains quite a lot of **great white sharks**.

AUSTRALIA

Great Australian Bight

Adelaide

Since the first South Australian colony was started in 1836, there have been **82 recorded incidents** of humans encountering sharks in a negative kind of way.

Only **20 of them** involved the person dying. That's an average of just one person every nine years.

Australian beach party: Page 94

How to defend yourself against a shark attack: Page 188

Shark-attack hotspots around the world: Page 138

Sharks do not think we are tasty

Most sharks don't like the taste of humans, so if they do take a bite out of you, they'll just swim away uninterested. Children do the same thing with their gran's **vegetable moussaka**.

Dinner is ready.

What is it?

It's called moussaka. Try it.

Has it got aubergines in it? I don't like aubergines.

No it hasn't got any aubergines in it. Well... not really. Although. Yes – it's mainly aubergine.

Right. I'm off.

Where are you going?

Somewhere where there is no moussaka you crumbling plimpturtle!

How much do sharks eat?: Page 100

How many sharks get eaten by people?: Page 55

Oceanic whitetip

Although oceanic whitetips are not as famous as great whites or tiger sharks, some people think they are the **most dangerous** type of shark.

SIZE: 3 metres long.

FAVOURITE FOOD: Sailors.

THIRD FUN FACT: They are afraid of Shirley Bassey.

It's difficult to tell how many people have been attacked by oceanic whitetips because most encounters happen out in the **open ocean**.

If you end up in a shipwreck and are floating around hanging on to a piano lid, these are the guys that are coming for you.

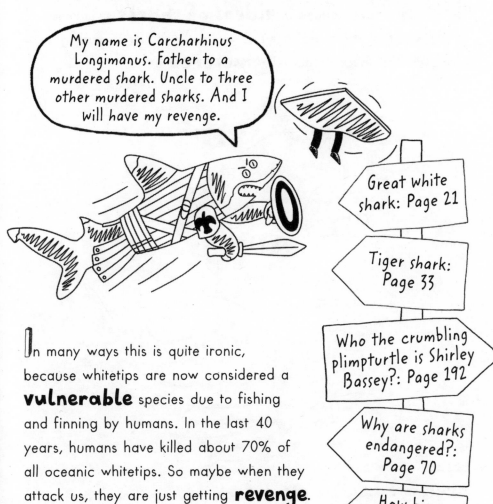

My name is Carcharhinus Longimanus. Father to a murdered shark. Uncle to three other murdered sharks. And I will have my revenge.

Great white shark: Page 21

Tiger shark: Page 33

Who the crumbling plimpturtle is Shirley Bassey?: Page 192

Why are sharks endangered?: Page 70

How big are sharks?: Page 60

In many ways this is quite ironic, because whitetips are now considered a **vulnerable** species due to fishing and finning by humans. In the last 40 years, humans have killed about 70% of all oceanic whitetips. So maybe when they attack us, they are just getting **revenge**.

Fish friends

You might have noticed in **videos of sharks** swimming in the wild that there are often some small fish just swimming alongside the shark or actually **suckered** on to it.

These fish are usually **pilot fish** (the ones that swim alongside) or **remora** (the suckery ones).

'What's going on here?' you might ask. 'Why doesn't the shark just make a quick turn and eat them up?'

Well, it turns out that what is going on here is a **mutualistic relationship**. Both the shark and fish help each other out.

The fish remove bits of **dead skin** from the shark and get rid of any parasites and nasty things that might be living on it. And in return the fish get to eat any leftover food that falls out of the shark's mouth, and more importantly get protection from their predators (who are afraid of sharks).

Shark spa day:
Page 156

Shark skin:
Page 92

Survival of
the fittest:
Page 140

So basically, these fishy friends are looked after by the shark in return for keeping it **clean and healthy**.

Nature is full of these relationships. It's not all survival of the fittest. In fact, some people say that there's not a lot of that at all.

Shark oil

Unlike other fish, sharks don't have a **swim bladder** to help them float. Instead they have a special oil in their liver which floats.

Without this they would sink to the bottom of the sea and not be able to get back up again, making them the most unsuccessful marine animal since the toffee fudge dolphin, which is now extinct, having been eaten by grandmothers all over the world.

Toffee fudge dolphin: Page 216

Weirdly, shark liver oil is used for medicinal purposes.

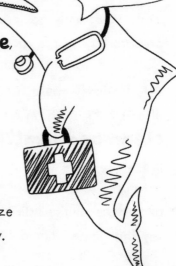

I said purposes! Not porpoises!

It contains a substance called **squalene,** which can be used to treat skin problems and even some sorts of cancer.

I don't know how they get the **oil out** of a shark. Maybe you can just carry

Anatomy of a shark: Page 69

a shark around with you and then give it a squeeze when you're feeling itchy.

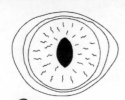 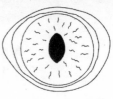

Shark eyes

Sharks have eyelids, but they don't use them because the seawater cleans their eyes as they swim around.

Some sharks have **'nictitating' eyelids**, which are see-through so they can close their eyes while still being able to see.

Cats have them too to protect their eyes when they are hunting or being attacked. I wonder if there are any other ways in which cats are like sharks ...

Why did you scratch me?

I'm so sorry – I thought you were a seal.

The **great white shark** doesn't have the ability to close its eyes. Instead, it rolls them back into its head when striking.

I wish I could roll my eyes back into my head. I'd be able to look at my brain and see what my imagination looks like from the outside.

Where is your imagination?: Page 43

Nice shark films

I can't find one movie about how brilliant sharks are. All the movies about sharks show them as killers, predators or genetically modified aliens. Sharks are never **the hero**.

So I've written an idea for a lovely, **cuddly** film about a lovely, cuddly shark. Imagine the scene:

TV shows about sharks: Page 36

Two princesses live alone in a castle. They hear strange noises coming from the watery dungeons and investigate. They find a beastly shark, who has been cursed until someone falls in love with him! He captures one princess, and even though he is a shark, she starts to **fall for him**.

But just at the moment they are about to kiss, she looks at his massive jagged teeth, the sloping fin, the cold dead eyes rolling back into his head, and the fact that he is zig-zagging towards her faster than a bus, and decides it would be a much better idea to **punch him** on the nose!

This really messes with his electro-receptors and he spirals out of the window into the sea below. The princess storms off into the mountains, where seven dwarf lantern sharks become her friends. They are called Bitey, Pointy, Finley, Frugal Sharkish, Sharka Khan, Unable-to-Sleepy and **Margaret**.

Just when we think everything is OK, the beastly shark appears from nowhere, silently stalks the other princess and then ...

Hang on! **Hang on!** Hang on!
This has got completely out of hand.

It's not possible to write a nice film about sharks. Maybe you should have a go.

Please email your ideas to:
outofofficeautomaticreply@canipleasejusthaveFIVEminutestomyself.net

Negative language used to describe sharks: Page 180

Bee nice: Page 30

The Jersey Shore shark attacks of 1916

Before 1916, people in the northern parts of the USA didn't really worry about sharks. People were getting bitten occasionally in Florida but it was very **rarely fatal** and, anyway, Florida has only been part of the USA since 1845.

Scientists believed that, even though there might be the odd accident here and there, no shark was strong enough to kill a human.

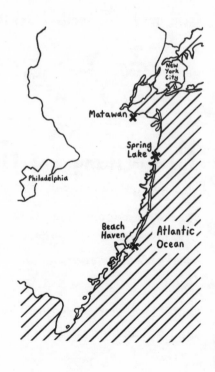

But then, in 1916, over the course of 12 days, **five people** were killed by sharks in four separate instances. All of them off the coast of New Jersey.

And this was the first time newspapers got really **hysterical** about sharks.

The problem is, of course, that newspapers don't always tell the truth. Their main purpose is to sell lots of newspapers.

If newspapers told you that this year's winter was going to be **terrible**, you'd worry about the weather and buy tomorrow's newspaper to find out more. If newspapers told you that people from Mars were all horrible, you would probably get angry at them. And if newspapers told you that sharks were **really scary**, then you might become scared of sharks.

DAILY SEA SNAIL

FREE BANANA WITH TODAY'S NEWSPAPER!

EXCLUSIVE: WHY WE DON'T LIKE MARS.

HOW CAN MARTIANS BE TRUSTED WHEN THEY'VE NEVER HEARD OF CHOCOLATE?

MARS BARRED

"I BET THEY HAVEN'T EVEN TRIED A MILKY WAY" SAYS CHOCOLATE SOURCE.

WINTER WILL BE TERRIBLE. PANIC NOW!

The summer of 1916 was really hot, and there had been an outbreak of a disease called polio in the New Jersey area. Everyone was told to go to the beach, get some fresh air and have a lovely swim.

Now, of course, the more people there are swimming in the sea, the more likely they are to bump into a shark. And if you bump into a great white or a bull shark, there is a chance that it will take **a bite** out of you.

So, five deaths from sharks in 12 days was probably a bit of a coincidence.

The newspapers, however, turned it into a huge event. Rewards were offered for killing the **'man-eating sharks'**. People wanted the government to spend money hunting sharks and building huge metal nets to keep sharks away from the shore.

For the first time in history, sharks were seen as dangerous, nasty and **evil**.

After 1916, because of the media hype, sharks were the bad guys! Sharks became something to be afraid of.

Even today, when someone gets bitten by a shark, it makes headlines all around the world. More people get killed by cows than sharks, but shark attacks make better headlines.

Jersey Shore cow massacre!: Page 215

Negative language used to describe sharks: Page 180

What's so scary about sharks?: Page 32

Sharks do not think we are tasty: Page 113

How many people get eaten by sharks?: Page 51

DAILY STAR
☆FISH☆
REWARD OFFERED TO CATCH KILLER SHARKS!

SCALY EXPRESS
BEWARE!

Maybe things would be different if there was a Jersey Shore **COW** massacre?

My Best Friend Is A Shark

Earlier this week in Skegness, Lincolnshire, an eight-year-old girl called Brandy Forklift stood on the steps of the aquarium and declared in a big voice:

'My best friend is called Trigger and he is a shark!'

Aquarium-Entrance

Brandy (who lives in Airedale, opposite the Airedale Air Museum) first met the four-foot-long blacktip reef shark when she was on a trip with her grandma to the Skegness Aquarium.

'Up until then,' says Brandy, 'all my friends were fluffy toys or imaginary unicorns that lived in my wardrobe. But when I saw those cold, dead eyes for the first time, I just knew that there was a beautiful soul hiding behind them.'

It turned out that the feeling was mutual, and Brandy and Trigger became penfriends, writing once a week to each other. Every

Shark eyes: Page 119

school holiday, Brandy makes the long journey from Yorkshire to Lincolnshire to visit her bestie. She spends all day sitting in front of the glass, feeding him fish and chips from Oh My Cod – the chippy round the corner.

'Sharks actually make really good BFFs,' says Brandy. 'He is really supportive, listens to all my problems and lets me pose for loads of selfies, even though he can't hold the phone cos he hasn't got thumbs.'

The Airedale Air Museum: Page 102

Blacktip reef shark: Page 167

Swimming with sharks: Page 232

Cookie-cutter shark

They are called cookie-cutter sharks because of the shape of their bite.

They don't eat whole fish. Or whole anything, really. What they do is swim up to whales and dolphins, attach themselves with their teeth

SIZE: 30 centimetres.

FAVOURITE FOOD: Bigger fish.

THIRD FUN FACT: They like singing songs about angry bananas.

and then twist around like a cookie-cutter, cutting out a chunk of flesh. Then they swim off, presumably **laughing** at the screams that are coming from the whale or dolphin.

Teeth marks made by cookie-cutters have been found on all sorts of whales, squid, people and even **submarines**.

Different types of shark attack: Page 184

But mostly, their bites don't usually kill the animal they've bitten.

So on the one hand, these are creepy, **horror-film** kind of creatures. On the other hand, maybe they've found a way to be meat eaters without actually killing anything.

This has given me a great idea for eating meat without killing any animals.

Instead of slaughtering a sheep, why not give it a general anaesthetic, amputate its leg, and then give it a false leg. The sheep can go back to wandering happily around the hills and you've got yourself a guilt-free leg of lamb for your Sunday roast.

129

Why is there so much plastic in the sea?

We have all heard that plastic in the ocean is a **huge problem**. But what is plastic? Why is it a problem? And how does it get in the sea?

We've been making plastic since the 1950s and, according to Greenpeace, since then all the plastic that has been made weighs about the same as **ONE BILLION ELEPHANTS!**

Trying to understand really big numbers: Page 194

Plastic is a really cheap way to make things. But the problem is that it doesn't ever go away. If you put a banana skin on your compost pile, it will get eaten by bacteria and worms. But bacteria and worms can't eat plastic. It's **indestructible**.

ONE BILLION ELEPHANTS

🐘 × 1,000,000,000

This is why we must re-use it, recycle it or just stop making the pagging stuff!

You've probably noticed that you have a special bin for recycling. And the plastic from your food packaging or toy packaging goes in there, and gets turned into something else. But only about 9% of the plastic we've created (that's 90 million elephants) has been recycled. The other **910 million** elephants'-worth of plastic is still out there, and a lot of it has ended up in the oceans.

I spoke to my friend Dr Alice Horton about this. She is a pollution scientist and works for the National Oceanography Centre. I asked what we could do about all the plastic. Could we maybe clean it up from the oceans?

She said that we can only see about 1% of the plastic: the pieces that are floating on the surface. But we don't know where the other 99% is. She reminded me that recently an underwater explorer called Victor Vescovo went 11 kilometres down to the bottom of the deepest trench in the oceans in a special submarine. He found all sorts of things that no one had seen before – BUT he also found a plastic bag ...

But how does plastic end up in the ocean?

Most of the plastic in the oceans has got there just from being litter. Someone puts a crisp packet in an overflowing bin. The wind blows it away, it goes down a drain and ends up in a river. And eventually all rivers go to the sea.

Microplastics are also polluting the oceans. These are **tiny bits of plastic** that have come off larger things like tyres and fishing equipment or little bits of synthetic clothing that come off in the washing machine.

These tiny bits of plastic get washed out to sea and cause **huge problems**. They get eaten by all kinds of sea creatures. Like whale sharks, which get their food by filtering huge amounts of seawater and pulling out plankton to eat. Dead marine animals are being found all around the world with huge lumps of plastic inside their stomachs.

There is probably even plastic in the fish you eat from the Oh My Cod fish and chip shop in your town.

We used to think that the seas were so big and deep that we could throw whatever we wanted into them and it wouldn't make any difference, like a **giant bin**. But now we know that all the plastic, together with the weather changes, are having a big impact for our oceans and everything that lives there.

OH MY COD
FISH & CHIPS

COD & CHIPS	5.99
SCAMPI & CHIPS	4.99
HADDOCK & CHIPS	6.99
FISHCAKE	1.50

FOOD ALLERGY WARNING
OUR FISH MAY CONTAIN PLASTIC

Why is there so much plastic in the sea?: Page 130

Whale shark: Page 86

My best friend is a shark: Page 126

What you can do to help endangered species: Page 224

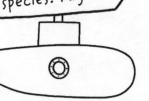

Scientists reckon that by 2050 there will be more plastic in the ocean than fish.

We can't expect the ocean to deal with this.

Shipwrecked Lego

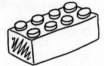

Lego is one of the best toys in the world. You can use it to make **anything** you like.

It is, however, made of plastic. This is fine when you keep it in a box and play with it, but one day in 1997 a lot of it went missing.

A container ship was hit by a **freak wave** while sailing 32 kilometres off the coast of Cornwall, causing 62 containers to fall off. One of these was carrying millions of pieces of Lego that still wash up on Cornish beaches today.

A lot of the Lego was themed around ships and pirates, so people sometimes find tiny octopuses and spearguns while building sandcastles.

Despite being bashed around in the ocean for decades, all the pieces of Lego are still in perfectly good condition. Because plastic is incredible. You can use it to make any shape and it will last **forever**.

We should probably be a lot more careful with it.

Rays

I love rays. My favourite ray is the one that runs the school in **Finding Nemo**.

Rays are not sharks, but they are very similar. Their skeleton is made from the same sort of cartilage as sharks. That's how they get to be so bendy and cool-looking.

SIZE: Up to 7 metres wide.

FAVOURITE FOOD: Plankton and the school dinner vegetarian option.

THIRD FUN FACT: They can weigh more than a car.

Some people say that a ray is like a **flat shark**. This would be handy if you wanted to post a shark. Posting a ray would be cheaper as it would get through a letterbox or under a door more easily.

The main difference between a shark and a ray is that sharks have their gills on the side and rays have their gills on their bottom. Having gills on your bottom would be **brilliant**.

Why aren't there any dangerous animals in the UK?

One of my favourite things about living in the UK is that I can go for a walk in the countryside with my children, and when we find a nice shady bit of grass under a tree we can sit down and watch the clouds drift by without worrying that some poisonous snake or spider is going to bite us on the **bottom**.

The only really dangerous animals in the UK are adders, bees and tiny dogs (if you've ever been bitten on the bottom by a terrier of some sort, you'll know what I mean). I got bitten by a **Jack Russell Sprout** one Christmas morning, and it was still hanging on to my bottom in February!

Wolves used to live in the wild in the UK. In Scotland, wolves were still considered to be a problem up until the 1700s. That's nearly tea time!

So why aren't there any wolves left in the wild in the UK? Well, the short answer is: we killed them all. People decided it was far too dangerous to have wolves wandering around, so various kings and queens gave bounty money to anyone who brought them wolf skins. And slowly but surely, all the wolves **disappeared**.

The Wolves of Yellowstone: Page 74

What you can do to help endangered species: Page 224

I hope the same thing doesn't happen to sharks.

Shark-attack hotspots around the world

Some beaches are more dangerous than others when it comes to shark encounters. I have listed the top five for you below. You'll notice, though, that even the most dangerous ones aren't actually very dangerous.

Daytona, FL: Page 42

ONE: Florida. In the last ten years, 244 people got bitten by sharks in Florida. Only one of them died. They were pretty cross, but most of them (mainly surfers) were back in the water as soon as their stitches healed.

TWO: Australia. In the same period of time, only 139 people got involved with a shark off the coast of Australia in a teeth-related rendezvous. But, sadly, 15 of them didn't

Where is Adelaide?: Page 112

make it back home. Most of these encounters involved great white sharks, which are **notoriously bitey**.

THREE: Hawaii.

Hawaii sharks: Page 178

There were 65 occasions in ten years when a shark and a person met up for lunch, and only two people died. It sounds like quite a lot for a small place. This is because the reefs around Hawaii are the perfect habitat for **tiger sharks.**

Tiger shark: Page 33

FOUR: South Africa. Same ten years: 41 attacks and 13 fatalities. Again, this is mainly because great white sharks are attracted to the growing seal population there.

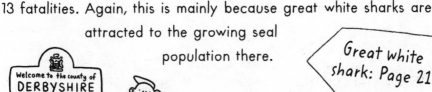

Great white shark: Page 21

FIVE: Derbyshire:

0 attacks. 0 fatalities.

Why aren't there any dangerous animals in the UK?: Page 136

Survival of the fittest

It has often been thought that animals and plants grow and improve by **competing** with each other. In a forest, surely the fastest-growing trees get more sunshine and become the tallest trees so they can look down at smaller trees and laugh at them Then they can grow more seeds and make more trees that are tall like them.

The fastest wolves get to their prey first, eat first, get bigger and stronger, become more attractive to other wolves and pass their faster, stronger genes on to their children.

Wow! She is awesome. I want to have puppies with her.

But the phrase **'survival of the fittest'** is often misunderstood.

Being the fittest in nature doesn't necessarily mean biggest, strongest or most aggressive. It can often be the best camouflaged, or the cleverest, or the one that gets on really well with others.

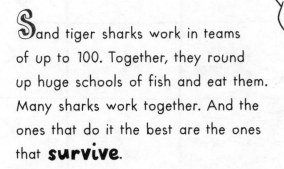

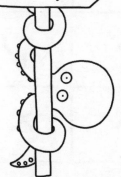

Wolves in Yellowstone: Page 74

Tiger shark: Page 33

How sharks do good in the ocean: Page 154

Sand tiger sharks work in teams of up to 100. Together, they round up huge schools of fish and eat them. Many sharks work together. And the ones that do it the best are the ones that **survive**.

We now know that trees in a forest actually **communicate** with each other using networks of fungi under the ground. They warn each other of threats like insects and disease. They even feed each other in times of need. It's not about each tree doing its best to be the fittest and survive: it's about **the whole forest**.

141

Different sharks

	Seals	Plankton	Bony fish and crabs
Great white shark	✔	✘	✔
Whale shark	✘	✔	✔
Lemon shark	✘	✘	✔
Tiger shark	✔	✘	✔
Blue shark	✔	✘	✔
Hammerhead shark	✔	✘	✔
Shirley Bassey	✘	✘	✘

different food

Turtles	Fish and smaller sharks	Squid	Rays	Cheese-and-onion crisps and rice cakes
✓	✓	✓	✓	✗
✗	✗	✗	✗	✗
✗	✓	✓	✓	✗
✓	✓	✓	✓	✗
✗	✓	✓	✗	✗
✗	✓	✓	✓	✗
✗	✗	✗	✗	✓

A funny story about voiceovers

Often, when I take Mrs Miggins, our family dog, for a walk, we bump into a stern-looking woman with a pile of Labradors. The first time we met, our conversation went like this:

ME: Hello.

LADY: What have you got there?

ME: A spaniel.

LADY: Does it work?

ME: Um ... yeah. It kind of works. You put food in one end and poo comes out ...

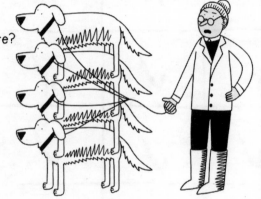

What she meant, of course, is that some dogs are trained as **working dogs**. Once I'd realised this, I explained that Mrs Miggins doesn't work, unless her job involved being cute and doing a wee on your shoes.

The thing is, though – a couple of years ago she did kind of get a job.

I was doing some voiceover work and took Mrs Miggins with me because she likes the adventure. She spent the whole day with the sound engineer, mainly sleeping, sometimes whacking herself in the face with her own ears and occasionally making whimpery, whiny sounds.

At the end of the day, the sound engineer asked me if he could record Mrs Miggins making sounds for a secret TV ad. So we put her on a stool and recorded her snuffling and whining and woofing and breathing.

I completely forgot all about it, **BUT** that Christmas, the sound engineer emailed to tell me the ad was on TV. It was for a well-known department store, and at the beginning you see some foxes sniffing around. But the noises they make are not really foxes: it's actually Mrs Miggins in the recording studio!

So the next time I saw the Labrador lady and she asked if Mrs Miggins worked, I said, 'Yes, she's a voiceover artist!'

TV shows about sharks: Page 36

TV shows for seals: Page 38

How many seas are there?

How many seas are there in the world? Well, there is the **North Sea**, the **Mediterranean Sea**, the **Indian Ocean**, the **Pacific Ocean** and loads of others.

In films about pirates, you sometimes hear people talk about '**the seven seas**'.

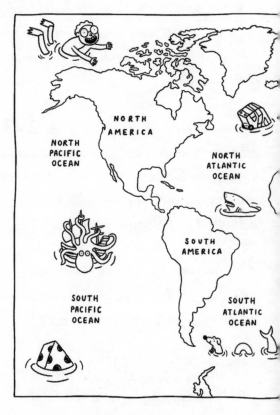

But really, if you think about it and look at a map, there is actually only one. You can talk about different bits of the ocean being called different things but they are all connected and are actually one massive body of water. It's called **The Ocean.**

NORTH AMERICA

NORTH PACIFIC OCEAN

NORTH ATLANTIC OCEAN

SOUTH AMERICA

SOUTH PACIFIC OCEAN

SOUTH ATLANTIC OCEAN

This is why some sharks manage to appear all over the world, swimming great distances.

How do sharks navigate?: Page 80

It's also how man-made pollution like **plastic** gets all over the place, even to uninhabited islands in the middle of nowhere.

When you do something to one part of the ocean, you do it to the **whole ocean**.

ARCTIC OCEAN

EUROPE

ASIA

AMERICA

PACIFIC OCEAN

INDIAN OCEAN

AUSTRALIA & OCEANIA

SOUTHERN OCEAN

Shark-attack hotspots around the world: Page 138

Where can you find sharks?: Page 20

Why is there so much plastic in the sea?: Page 130

But how does plastic end up in the ocean?: Page 132

Collective nouns

The collective noun for sharks is a 'shiver'. A shiver of sharks.

Collective nouns are words used to describe groups of things.

Some of them you can use for anything, like 'bunch' or 'load': a bunch of sausages, a load of angry bananas.

But some things have particular collective nouns that are especially for them. They tell you about the thing they are describing and help paint a picture of them in your head.

Here are some of my favourites. (Some of them might be made-up.)

A ream of paper

A gaggle of geese

An index of librarians

A pack of thieves

A galaxy of lollipop ladies

A murder of crows

A cabbage of dinner ladies

A powerpoint of supply teachers

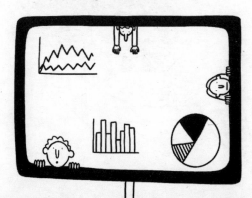

Can you keep pet sharks?

NO!

They are wild animals.

My best
friend is a shark:
Page 126

What are
sharks?:
Page 16

Ten things
you didn't know
about sharks:
Page 205

Mako sharks

Mako sharks mostly live around the islands of **Hawaii**.

There are two types. Long-fin makos and short-fin makos. The long-fins are about 2 metres long. The short-fins are only half that size, BUT they are officially the **fastest** sharks in the ocean.

Some people say they can move at about **95 kmph**.

If a shark travelled at 95 kmph down a street where the speed limit is 50 kmph and the police caught it, it would be **arrested** and have its driving licence taken away for a year.

If mako sharks could ride scooters, they would be banned from shopping malls.

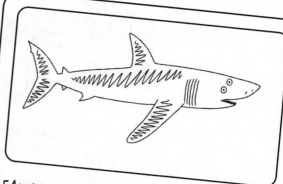

FAVOURITE FOOD: Fish, particularly tuna, but I have no idea how they open the tins.

FUN FACT: The most popular name for a mako shark is Usain.

Anatomy of a shark: Page 69

Hawaii sharks: Page 178

Things we are afraid of and why

Imagine something that someone might be **afraid** of, and I bet that someone out there really is afraid of it.

But what are the most common ones?

Claustrophobia is the fear of small spaces. People with claustrophobia don't like playing sardines, being a magician's assistant or being stuck in a lift.

Nyctophobia is a fear of the dark. Lots of people are afraid of the dark. But it's the things that are hiding in the dark that you should be afraid of. Things like sharks on scooters and really angry bananas.

Acrophobia is a fear of heights. People with a proper fear of heights are afraid of heights even when they are not particularly high up.

If you think about it, being afraid of heights is irrational. The height itself can't hurt you. It's falling. **Falling** is what you should be worried about! Actually, falling is probably quite good fun once you get used to it. Landing! Landing is the bit that's going to cause you problems.

But **phobias** don't often make sense. It doesn't make sense to be afraid of sharks because the chances that they will hurt you are ridiculously slim. So why are we afraid?

Irrational fear of sharks: Page 98

How I got over my phobia of sharks: Page 104

If you have any sort of fear of anything at all, it's probably a good idea to tell a grown-up about it, or read a book about it, unless you're afraid of **books**...

In which case put the book down, run away screaming, and then go and tell a grown-up about it.

How sharks do good in the ocean

Sharks have a really **important** job in the ocean. They are almost always an 'apex predator', which means that there are no other animals that are hunting them. And it is a shark's job to manage the populations of animals that they eat. If for some reason there are suddenly loads of fish, then the shark population will increase to eat more of them and bring the balance back.

But sharks are even **cleverer** than that. Because they have to chase their prey, they tend to catch and eat the slower, older, poorly ones. The super-fit fish get away and get to pass their genes on. So sharks are helping to keep the ecosystem healthy.

BLUE MARLIN

Survival of the fittest: Page 140

They also keep things that they don't eat healthy, like **sea grass**. Tiger sharks, for example, eat a lot of turtles. And turtles eat a lot of sea grass. Because turtles are always looking out for tiger sharks, they don't sit around all day eating all the sea grass. They munch a bit, and then swim on. So the sea grass has time to recover from being munched.

Tiger shark: Page 33

I do a similar thing with tomato plants. Every time I pick some tomatoes from my garden, I choose the biggest, healthiest-looking ones and save the seeds from inside them. I use these seeds to grow next year's plants. This way my tomatoes will get better and better each year.

Eventually my tomatoes are going to be **so big** and healthy that I worry one of them will eat me!

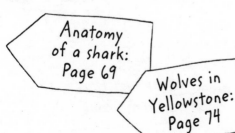

Anatomy of a shark: Page 69

Wolves in Yellowstone: Page 74

Something that hunts great whites: Page 174

Shark Spa Day

Being a shark can be very stressful, and they mainly smell of fish. This is why they often get together with some friends and visit a **shark spa**.

These usually happen in the posh parts of a reef, somewhere lovely and warm. The sharks have skin scrubs (when **remora** eat the dead skin off their backs), relax in Jacuzzis (where other sharks blow water all over their faces with their buccal pumping), and enjoy massages (hundreds of tiny crabs run all over them singing songs).

Fish friends: Page 116

I've never actually been to one of these spa days, but they sound great!

Making things up just to sound funny: Page 182

The Sharks from West Side Story

West Side Story is a brilliant musical version of **Romeo and Juliet**, written by Leonard Bernstein and Stephen Sondheim.

In Shakespeare's play, the two feuding families are called the Montagues and the Capulets. In **West Side Story**, they are the Jets and the Sharks.

The two gangs sing brilliant songs about how horrible the other gang is, and talk about having a **rumble** a lot. A rumble is when you use dancing instead of fighting.

> We gotta stay away from those Sharks, Riff.

> Yeah. That kick-turn-kick move is really deadly.

If you ever end up in a situation where someone wants to fight with you, try **dancing** instead. In fact, any difficult situation can usually be solved by dancing.

The Grammarhead Shark

I am the Grammarhead Shark, and I find it really annoying when people say the following things:

Moving forwards: Page 40

Moving forwards.
Basically.
Like.

As in, 'Moving forwards, can I basically get like more milkshakes?'

Do you want more milkshakes or do you want something that is **like** more milkshakes but isn't more milkshakes? Make up your mind!

I also really hate it when people say **less** instead of **fewer**. If something can be counted in units of some kind and you take some of them away, you have fewer, not less.

When my local supermarket put up a sign above the till saying **'10 items or less'**, I demanded to speak to the manager,

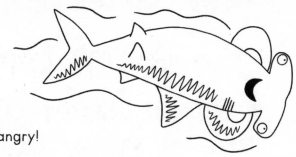

and when he came out from behind his cowardly counter I bit his leg! Bad grammar makes me really angry!

A couple of years ago, though, a **whale shark** suggested I calm down and stop criticising other people so much. The things we find annoying about other people are usually things that we do ourselves in some way. I get annoyed when people use words wrong because I do it all the time. I'm a shark. I'm still learning how to write in **proper sentences**.

These days, if someone says 'less' instead of 'fewer', I just **tut** silently inside my own head and then give myself a bonus point for not correcting them.

BUT! When I see a sign at the greengrocer like this:

Potato's Half Price

Then I say, 'Oi, greengrocer! There is no apostrophe in potatoes! Do it again and I will bite your arm off!'

Whale shark: Page 86

Making things up just to sound funny: Page 182

159

Things that are more likely to kill you than sharks

If you are afraid of sharks, this page may help. Many more people are killed by lightning than are killed by sharks. Apparently, you are also more likely to be killed by your **toaster** than a shark!

Although that's probably because most people have a toaster in the corner of their kitchen. If everyone had a bull shark on the worktop between the bread bin and the blender, there would probably be more shark deaths than there are at the moment.

Would a shark kill you if it landed on your head?: Page 90

To do list
Buy milk
Feed shark

BREAD

So here is a list of things that are statistically more likely to kill you than a shark.

BEING HIT ON THE HEAD BY A COCONUT – 150 PEOPLE PER YEAR

Yes, that's right. Sitting under a **coconut tree** seems to be more dangerous than being out in the surf with the sharks.

Extreme coconuts: Page 200

MOSQUITOES CARRYING MALARIA – 800,000 PEOPLE PER YEAR

These guys are not just annoying. In many parts of the world, mosquitoes transmit **malaria**, which can be a deadly illness.

CHAMPAGNE CORKS – 25 PEOPLE PER YEAR

Apparently, corks travel quite quickly and if one hits you right between the eyes you won't be drinking any more champagne. Or drinking anything. Or doing anything.

HORSES - 20 PEOPLE PER YEAR

The trick is not to get kicked by a horse. Or trodden on. And don't fall off one, either, and land **on your head** in a pool of sharks!

SMOKING - 8,000,000 PEOPLE PER YEAR

Surely we all know now that smoking is really, **really** bad for you.

HIPPOS - 3,000 PEOPLE PER YEAR IN AFRICA

Most people who are killed by hippos die because they drive their car into a hippo. Apparently, hippos have a habit of standing in the middle of the road at night and it's quite easy to accidentally drive your car into one. But that's not the hippo's fault. Those people haven't been killed by a hippopotamus. They have been killed by their car.

If you ride your scooter into a **lollipop lady**, you haven't been attacked by a lollipop lady!

FALLING OUT OF BED – 450 PEOPLE PER YEAR IN THE USA

Don't start worrying about falling out of bed. I phoned my physicist godson David again, and he says that if you were to fall out of a standard-sized bed, by the time it took you to hit

the carpet you would be travelling at a dizzying 3 kmph. So you'll probably be OK. All of those 450 people who died were really old. Older people are extremely brittle.

VENDING MACHINES – 2 PEOPLE PER YEAR IN THE USA

Vending-nado: Page 214

You know those machines that sell chocolate bars and stuff? You have to put in the right code, and then it makes brilliant whirring noises and the thing you want falls out of the bottom? Well, apparently, every now and again they randomly fall over and squash people. Although I think it's likely that what actually happens is that two people per year get really angry with the machine because it won't give them the chocolate bar they want. They then have a fight with the vending machine and the vending machine wins.

TAKING A SELFIE – 250 PEOPLE PER YEAR

Yes! **Vanity** and showing off online can be really bad for your health. You really have to be careful with your phone. Don't be tempted to take a selfie doing something silly or standing somewhere dangerous. I don't know if anyone has ever been killed by a shark while posing for a selfie.

My phobia of sharks: Page 82

Bull shark: Page 101

How I got over my phobia of sharks: Page 104

MESSY HANDWRITING – 1,200 PEOPLE PER YEAR

I know! There is a reason your teachers make you spend hours learning how to do joined-up cursives as a way to help you prepare for the digital world.

1,200 people a year die because pharmacists can't read what doctors have written on prescriptions, so they give you the wrong medicine!

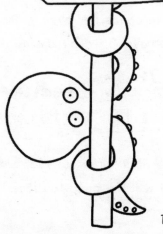

Trying to understand really big numbers: Page 194

Things we don't love and wouldn't save if they were endangered: Page 172

How many people get eaten by sharks?: Page 51

Why grown-ups rest their eyes

You're sitting with your grandma watching the latest **Star Wars** film. You look over to see if she's enjoying herself as much as you are. But she's **not** watching it. She has her eyes closed and small farty-snoring noises are coming out of her nose.

Shark eyes: Page 119

Moving forwards: Page 40

'Nan!' you yell. 'Why are you asleep?'

She opens her eyes, stares awkwardly for a couple of seconds, and says, 'I wasn't asleep. I'm just **resting** my eyes.'

What? Surely **bedtime** is for resting your eyes? Not the middle of the afternoon, watching the most exciting film ever made!

Well, it turns out that old people sometimes get very tired eyes, and feel the need to close them.

Blacktip reef shark

These beautiful sharks live in shallow, **tropical waters** around reefs in the Indian and Pacific Oceans.

They tend to stay in one area all of their lives. They don't **migrate** or anything. They just swim around their reef, hunting for fish.

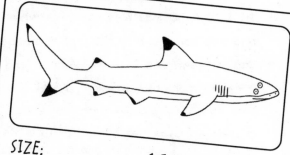

SIZE: 1.5 metres long.

FAVOURITE FOOD: Fish.

THIRD FUN FACT: Widely considered the most beautiful sharks in the world.

They have black tips on the end of their fins. Presumably, when it came to naming these sharks, scientists just looked at each other and went:

My best friend is a shark: Page 126

What shall we call this shark that lives on a reef?

The one that has black tips on their fins? yes.

How about we call them black tip reef sharks and then go get donuts?

Whatever.

Loan sharks

A loan shark is someone who will lend you some money. It's not someone who will lend you a shark. Why would someone want to borrow a shark?

> I'm a bit skint this week. Can you lend me two reef sharks and a whitetip?

Let's say your car breaks down. It's going to cost £200 to fix it. You haven't got £200.

What will you do? Come to me, the loan shark. I'll give you the £200, you can get your car fixed. And then all you have to do is pay me back £100 per month for **the rest of your life**.

And if you're not able to pay me ... there will be consequences.

Where is your imagination?: Page 43

Making things up just to sound funny: Page 182

Frugal Sharkish

He is a singing shark from Northern Ireland and was the lead singer of the pop punk band **The Wondersharks**.

They sang a brilliant song called 'I'm Covered In Spots and I Hang Out Down the Bus Stop', which is very famous. And loads of others which I've never heard of, including, 'You've Got my Fishy Chicken: Why Don't You Eat It?'

In 1985, Frugal Sharkish became the Director of the Airedale Air Museum in Yorkshire, where he was responsible for looking for **new Farts** from Famous People. He found it really easy to get fart donations of inferior quality and is responsible for the exhibition of **Lesser Bum Trumpets** that you can still go and see today and his hit song 'A Good Fart Is Hard to Find'.

The Airedale Air Museum: Page 102

Frugal is now a hugely respected **campaigner** for cleaning up Britain's rivers.

What can you do to help endangered species?: Page 224

Megamouth shark

This shark has officially the most **awesome** name of any shark. Any animal that has 'mega' in its name has to be one of my favourites.

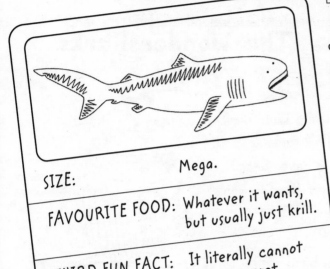

SIZE:	Mega.
FAVOURITE FOOD:	Whatever it wants, but usually just krill.
THIRD FUN FACT:	It literally cannot keep a secret.

Megamouth sharks are deep-water sharks, and are so rare that they were only discovered by humans in 1976. Only about **100 megamouths** have ever been seen or caught.

They are quite similar to whale sharks and basking sharks in that they swim along catching plankton. Megamouths are smaller than either of those sharks, but they have massive mouths and **rubbery lips**.

I've tried to find other animals with **'mega'** in their name and there aren't any. Maybe in the future, though, we can genetically modify animals to make them **really large**.

Shark teeth:
Page 28

Different
sharks/different
food: Page 142

How big
are sharks?:
Page 60

I would particularly like to meet a mega-cow, a mega-hamster and a **mega-mouthed duck**.

Things we don't love and wouldn't save if they were endangered

According to the **World Wildlife Fund**, we really don't know how many species are going extinct every year because there are loads of things that we don't even know exist.

Scientists estimate that between 200 and 2,000 different types of animal become **extinct** each year. That's a lot.

When you see a picture of a terrified **orang-utan** clinging to a digger that's just destroyed its home, it's easy to feel sorry for it and decide you'll never eat palm oil again. But this is partly because orang-utans look a bit like people. And some people look a bit like orang-utans. And orang-utans look really cute and cuddly.

What can you do to help endangered species?: Page 224

It's much harder to care about some ugly-looking **beetle** that no one has ever heard of.

There are animals where I live that I probably wouldn't care about if they were endangered.

Survival of the fittest: Page 140

Slugs – they eat things in my vegetable garden.

Wasps – they ruin picnics.

Flies – they wake my wife up in the middle of the night and I have to chase them round the bedroom trying to kill them with a book.

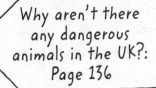

Even though all of these creatures are extremely annoying, I'm sure that they have their place in the ecosystem and are just as important as **Siberian tigers** and **green turtles**.

Why aren't there any dangerous animals in the UK?: Page 136

Something that hunts great whites

An **'apex predator'** is an animal that eats other animals but doesn't have any predators of its own so doesn't need to worry about being hunted.

Like the **Komodo dragon** in Indonesia. Because it has no predators, it spends most of its time just wandering around the beach, looking mean and awesome.

For years, everyone thought that great white sharks were apex predators too. Surely there could be nothing that would take them on ...

But in 2016, people found dead great white sharks on the beach in False Bay, which is near Cape Town, South Africa. And these deaths coincided with a pod of **killer whales**, or orca, turning up in the bay.

The theory among whale experts is that **orca** have learned how to take on a great white. They'll give the shark a bash with their tail, stunning it, then they flip it over on to its back. If a shark goes on its back it goes into a kind of sleep. A bit like a **trance**. The same thing happens when you tickle a dog's tummy.

Once the orca has immobilised the shark, it simply bites the shark just below its pectoral fin, and then **sucks out** its liver!

A shark's liver is full of oil, which has lots of calories and goodness. We use it for all sorts of things. So maybe orca have worked out that this is a good way to keep themselves healthy. And they're telling their friends about it too, because it's happening **all over the oceans!**

Great white shark: Page 21

Shark-attack hotspots around the world: Page 138

Shark oil: Page 118

How many seas are there?: Page 146

Hawaii sharks

I read somewhere that Hawaiian culture really respects sharks, so I contacted the lovely people at Hawaii Shark Encounters and asked them if they had any stories about this. They sent me an article by Herb Kawainui Kāne, who is **a living treasure**.

He says that many people believe their dead ancestors can return to them in the form of sharks and help them by chasing a fish into their net or by guiding them home when they are lost in a canoe.

Mako shark: Page 151

What you can do to help endangered species: Page 224

Because of this belief, the people of Hawaii would never harm or eat a shark. To do so would be hugely disrespectful and would probably cause sickness and accidents to happen to you. There are even stories of village elders taking food down to the sea in the evening, calling to

a shark and then feeding it.

Maybe if more people had this attitude to sharks, they might not be so endangered. If we treated all sharks like they might be members of our family, would that make the world a **better place?**

I do a similar thing with all blue cars. I never overtake a blue car just in case it's my mum. She gets **road rage** like nothing you've ever seen before.

Negative language used to describe sharks

People who write articles about shark bites tend to use really **negative language** to make it sound more exciting.

If you say, 'Human-munching Monster Shark Attacks Surfer,' more people are likely to read it. It's not really fair to use the word 'attack', though, unless you can be sure that the shark deliberately chose to bite someone.

If you accidentally stand on a shark's head and it bites you, were you attacked by a shark or was it just an **accident**?

If you are swimming and a shark takes a bite to see what you taste like, have you been attacked, or is this just an **unfortunate encounter** with wildlife?

Here are some better ways to describe what happens when people encounter sharks and their teeth:

The Jersey Shore shark attacks of 1916: Page 122

Do sharks sleep?: Page 78

Sharks do not think we are tasty: Page 113

How to avoid being mistaken for lunch: Page 206

181

Making things up just to sound funny

The other day I was in a primary school, and one of the children said he had a pet turkey. I thought this was a **bit weird** ...

It turned out, though, that he was just making things up to **sound funny**.

Where is your imagination?:
Page 43

Making things up just to sound funny is lots of fun, but you do have to be **careful** to get it right.

For example, if a police officer asks you where you were on Friday night between midnight and 2 a.m., don't say you were robbing the Crown Jewels from the Tower of London with your gang of illegal alligators just to sound funny. You may end up in **prison**.

My job is 90% making things up just to sound funny, and 20% maths.

I think the trick is to make sure what you've made up is **actually funny**. Often you do your best, but it turns out that what you said was only funny to you. If you make something up and no one laughs, just do what I do and keep adding more and more nonsense, getting stranger and stranger until someone eventually does a **chuckle-fart**.

Toaster shark: Page 201

Different types of shark attack

Now, even though this is incredibly **rare**, every now and again, a normally friendly shark might decide that you are food.

There are **three main ways** that sharks attack people. Some sharks are working on a fourth way, which involves dangling from your bedroom ceiling, but the science on this is blurry.

HIT-AND-RUN ATTACKS

The shark takes a little bite, decides that you're not worth eating, and swims off. These happen really quickly and often in murky water. The shark mistakes you for something that it usually eats. As soon as it tastes you, it realises that you don't contain enough calories to justify the effort. So it swims off. Most people don't even see the shark. They feel the bite, but assume they must have scraped their leg on a rock or something. It's only when they get back to the beach that they notice the **teeth-shaped wound**.

BUMP-AND-BITE ATTACKS

This is how sharks decide if you are dinner or not.

The shark gives you a bump with its nose, or a cheeky little bite, and then circles you trying to decide if you're going to be easy to eat. If it thinks you're worth the risk, it comes in for the kill.

If you find yourself being a recipient of a **bump and bite**, turn to page 188 to find out what to do.

How to defend yourself against a shark attack: Page 188

Shark-attack hotspots around the world: Page 138

SNEAK ATTACK

You won't know this is happening until it happens. And it will be over almost immediately. The shark comes at you from below and kills fairly **swiftly**. This is how great whites catch seals, moving at almost 50 kmph when they strike. That's like being hit by a car – with teeth. This only happens if the shark thinks you are a seal or a smaller shark.

How to avoid being mistaken for lunch: Page 206

Retrieving bricks from the bottom of the pool in your pyjamas

One of the **weirdest things** that might happen when learning to swim is a test where you have to get a brick from the bottom of the pool while wearing your pyjamas.

Everyone always says, 'What's the point of this?'

BUT – a couple of weeks ago I was staying in a hotel with an outdoor swimming pool. In the morning, while still wearing my pyjamas, I heard a woman crying by the pool. She had dropped her **pet brick** into the pool and it had sunk to the bottom!

'My brick,' she wailed. 'My beautiful brick.'

As quick as a flash, I dived into the pool and rescued the brick. **Hurray!**

186

Of course, the **brick test** is really just to see if you are a strong swimmer. So I've made up some other brilliant ways that would test if you are a good swimmer without ruining a perfectly good pair of jammies.

1. Swim one length backstroke while holding a plushy toy shark in your teeth. If the shark gets wet, you are **disqualified**.

2. Swim to the bottom of the pool while wearing a shark costume, and pretend to be a sleeping **nurse shark**.

3. Get dressed in the swimming-pool changing rooms without getting your socks wet.

4. Swim a width underwater while wearing a **shark onesie** with your eyes closed without accidentally swimming into an old lady's bum.

Blake Chapman: Page 220

Cheating at swimming races: Page 212

Something worse than sharks: Page 196

How to defend yourself against a shark attack – myths and truths

Ask anyone how to defend against a shark, and you'll hear lots of suggestions.

For this section, I have used the advice written by shark expert Blake Chapman from her excellent book **Shark Attacks**.

If you become the star attraction in a bump-and-bite scenario, the shark will first bump you with its nose. This will hurt because shark skin is sharp.

Then the shark will circle around you, deciding whether to attack. If it does, you will notice some signs that you are in a **lot of trouble**:

Blake Chapman: Page 220

Shark skin: Page 92

1. The shark is coming directly towards you quickly, possibly zig-zagging, with its fin sloping backwards.

 2. People around you are screaming and using rude words.

 3. Its head is rising upwards.

 4. Its mouth is open, and you are not a dentist.

 5. You suddenly need an unscheduled poo.

Most shark attacks involve a shark **biting your legs** and hanging on, because legs are dangly and easy to grab hold of.

The Sharks from West Side Story: Page 157

You probably have five seconds to convince the shark to let go before the whole thing has got completely out of hand.

This has gone beyond funny now.

But you can't **talk** your way out of this situation. And this is not the right time for some dance fighting.

You have to take direct and aggressive action.

A lot of people say you should **punch the shark** on its nose until it lets go. But that's extremely hard to do if the shark has got its teeth around your leg. Plus, the shark's nose skin is super tough and sharp, and will cut your hands.

If you are holding some sort of a weapon – a spear, a flipper or a hammer – use that instead. My favourite anti-shark weapon is a DeWalt Brushless 18V Lithium-Ion Keyless Cordless Drill Driver. But they don't work underwater.

Things that should not be in this book: Page 236

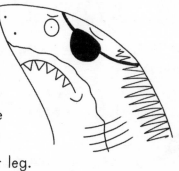

Other people say it's better to aim for either the shark's eye or gills.

The shark needs these to stay alive, so if you can damage one of them, the shark will probably decide you are not worth attacking and will let go of your leg. Get your fingers into its eye, jab them right round the sides and pull out its eyeball.

You are probably thinking that this is **totally gross**, and it is. But it's not as gross as having your leg bitten off.

Once the shark decides to let go of you, the next thing to do is to get out of the water as quickly as possible before it comes back with its mates.

BUT REMEMBER: YOU ARE EXTREMELY UNLIKELY TO GET ATTACKED BY A SHARK. IT ALMOST NEVER HAPPENS.

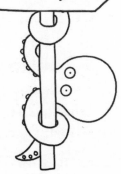

How many people get eaten by sharks?: Page 51

Shark eyes: Page 119

How to avoid being mistaken for lunch: Page 206

Who the crumbling plimpturtle is Shirley Bassey?

Dame Shirley Veronica Bassey is one of Britain's **best loved** elderly singers.

Born in 1937, this gloriously wind-piped pensioner sang **three** theme songs to Bond films:

Goldfinger
Diamonds Are Forever
Moonraker

More people each year die doing impressions of Shirley Bassey than are killed by sharks. That's why some people are so afraid of her ...

Different sharks/different food: Page 142

Things that are more likely to kill you than sharks: Page 160

Things that should not be in this book: Page 236

School shark

Imagine a shark that you can take to school with you.

Actually, no. That's not what a school shark is.

School sharks like to swim around in schools of other school sharks. That's how they got their name.

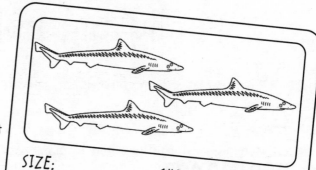

SIZE: 140 centimetres.

FAVOURITE FOOD: Sardines.

THIRD FUN FACT: An inspector had one for his lunch and said it was outstanding.

You can find school sharks in all sorts of places, particularly the North Atlantic and the Mediterranean.

Lots of them get eaten by people as apparently they are particularly tasty and easy to catch.

If you catch one, take it to school with you. See what happens.

Who is eating all these sharks and why?: Page 62

How many sharks get eaten by people?: Page 55

Collective nouns: Page 148

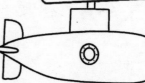

Trying to understand really big numbers

When it comes to understanding sharks, there are lots of big numbers involved.

The number of sharks eaten by humans in a year is **100,000,000**.

And sharks have been on Earth for **450,000,000** years.

These numbers are so massive that it's really difficult to understand them. One way to make them easier to understand is by working out how many seconds each one is.

A million seconds is 11½ years.
A billion seconds is 32 years.
A trillion seconds is 32,000 years.

How many sharks get eaten by people?: Page 55

The chances of being eaten by a shark are approximately one in one hundred and fifty thousand million.

That's **1 in 150,000,000,000**.

How many people get eaten by sharks?: Page 51

Sharks are really old: Page 48

That's an incredibly big number too, so the chances are incredibly small. But lots of people are still afraid that it might happen to them.

One of the reasons that people are afraid of shark attacks is that human beings find it much easier to understand yes or no questions.

When someone says that there is a **1-in-150,000,000,000** chance of being bitten by a shark, we don't really know what that means. So our brains change the sum. It changes it to answering a yes or no question: 'Is there a possibility that I will be bitten by a shark?' And the answer, of course, is YES. It is possible.

Something worse than sharks

You might have noticed that the worst thing about being a kid is that often your face is the same height as **a grown-up's bum**.

This is really annoying. Just walking through a room full of grown-ups is a nightmare, especially if they've all just eaten big bowls of lentils and broccoli.

How many times have you accidentally walked into a grown-up's bum **with your face?**

It often happens in a queue. You're facing the wrong way, talking to your brother, the queue moves and your dad tells you to catch up, you turn around and whoooomph! You just walked into someone's bum – with your face.

Is it worse running into a stranger's bum or your mum's bum?

Like when your mum is trying to find something in the cupboard under the sink, and you come running into the kitchen to get a glass of water at full speed. But you're going too fast. You can't stop. You see this massive mum-bum looming towards you! And before you know it, BOOM! You've high-fived your mum's bum with your face.

It's literally the **worst**.

A shark, however, would never accidentally swim into its mum's bum because they have electro-reception, which enables them to detect objects without actually seeing them.

How do sharks navigate?: Page 80

Things that are more likely to kill you than sharks: Page 160

Frugal Sharkish: Page 169

What sharks are like when they are old

Some sharks live until they are about **130 years old**, but no one is sure exactly how old they can be. This is because whenever scientists have found a really old shark and they've asked the shark how old it is, the shark has replied:

> 'I can't remember, dearie. Are you my Auntie Barbara?'

When sharks get old, they go and live in special **shark homes** for the elderly which are always by the sea. There is an electric chairlift to help them get from the bottom of the ocean to the top of reefs. There is also a shark mobility jet-ski so that those sharks whose fins don't work so well any more can still get around.

> What did you do in the war, Grandpa?

> Well, I was involved with the USS Indianapolis ...

Old sharks also have all the **best stories**. You just have to take the time to sit and listen to them.

The oldest shark

The oldest type of shark that is still around today is the goblin shark, which is reckoned to be about 120 million years old. However, I read that in a book that was written in 1981 so by now that shark would be **120,000,040** years old. That's really old.

If you think about it, **the dinosaurs** were on our planet between 245 million and 66 million years ago, so that means there were sharks swimming in the oceans when there were dinosaurs on the land.

Sharks are **incredibly wise** old things. We surely have a lot to learn from them.

But not how to stay awake through an **entire film**.

Sharks are really old: Page 48

Why grown-ups rest their eyes: Page 166

Extreme coconuts

Every year, 150 people get killed by **coconuts**.

You are more likely to be killed by a coconut landing on your head than you are to have **a negative experience** with one of our shark friends.

Think about that: it's probably more dangerous to stay on the beach than it is to go in the water!

Things that are more likely to kill you than sharks: Page 160

How many sharks get eaten by people?: Page 55

BLENDER SHARK

There are over **500** different types of shark out there in the waters. But I thought it would be good to make a few up as well.

The **blender shark** likes to eat small fish and bananas. It sucks them into its conical mouth and then blends them together into a kind of smoothie with its rotating teeth.

TOASTER SHARK

More people are killed by their toaster every year than they are by sharks, so the **toaster shark** just confuses things even more.

This strange fish has gills that glow red-hot from eating lava in underwater **volcanoes**.

It is able to put five slices of bread into each gill to make toast for breakfast. The only problem is that the bread gets all soggy and disgusting. **Gross.**

Cookie-cutter shark: Page 128

Making things up just to sound funny: Page 182

Primal fear

There are different types of fear.

Rational fear is the sort of thing that is swayed by maths and common sense. For example, I have looked at the numbers and found that riding a scooter while blindfolded is statistically dangerous, so I'm not going to do it.

OR, it is extremely unlikely that I'm going to get squashed by a vending machine so I won't avoid using vending machines.

Why I avoid vending machines: Page 204

(Actually, I do avoid using vending machines. But not because they're dangerous – because they're pagging annoying!)

There is also **emotional or irrational fear.**

This comes from a part of our brain used by prehistoric humans, who were living in caves, eating woolly mammoths and saying 'ugg' all the time. At this time, humans could be attacked at any moment by wolves, bears or giant poisonous hedgehogs, so their brains would sound a little alarm and they'd run away.

Irrational fear of sharks: Page 98

Are you afraid of sharks?: Page 24

When we see a video of a shark with its fin back and its teeth out, this **anti-predator alarm** kicks in and makes us afraid.

The mathematical bit of our brain is a lot slower to react, so by the time it has told us that the shark is nothing to worry about, our anti-predator brain has run around shouting and screaming in panic.

My phobia of sharks: Page 82

This is **primal fear.**

It doesn't matter what you tell that part of your brain. It doesn't understand maths or statistics. It likes jumping, hiding under the duvet and causing unexpected **sudden poo situations**.

Why I avoid vending machines

Vending machines are really annoying!

They never have what I want.

Things that are more likely to kill you than sharks: Page 160

If they do have what I want, they won't let me have it.

I can see the bottle of blackcurrant cordial. I'm pressing the button for a bottle of blackcurrant cordial. But I can't have my bottle of blackcurrant cordial.

Because the vending machine is doing **absolutely nothing!**

Two people every year are killed by vending machines.

But I do not fear vending machines.

Vending machines should fear ME!!!!

Vending-nado!: Page 214

Ten things you didn't know about sharks

1. Sharks are afraid of cucumbers.

2. The first shark to climb Mount Everest did so in 1973 – without oxygen.

3. My mum's middle name is **'The Shark'**.

4. During the Battle of Trafalgar, sailors called sharks 'pointy wimble fish'.

5. Most sharks are called **Margaret**.

6. No shark has ever been to university.

7. Keeping a shark in a shoebox is illegal.

8. Some sharks have special pockets behind their pectoral fins in which they keep their locker key and a packet of tissues in case of emergency.

9. Tiger sharks are real. Shark tigers are not.

10. Reef sharks **whistle** when they are doing a poo.

How to avoid being mistaken for lunch

Nobody wants to be eaten by a shark. No one wants to be eaten by anything, really!

So if you want to play in the water in parts of the world where potentially dangerous sharks live, how can you reduce the risk of meeting a shark **teeth first?**

Here is some advice from Blake Chapman's excellent book **Shark Attacks**.

How to defend yourself against a shark attack: Page 188

Blake Chapman: Page 220

1. DO NOT SWIM IN AREAS WHERE THERE ARE KNOWN TO BE DANGEROUS SHARKS

This seems pretty obvious to me. Similarly, if you want to avoid being run over, stay away from roads.

2. ALWAYS SWIM WITH OTHER PEOPLE

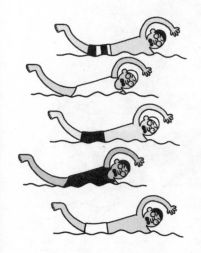 

Sharks clearly don't want to get involved in a fight with loads of people. Being in a group is probably safer.

3. DO NOT SWIM IN DIRTY WATER

This is because a shark is more likely to mistake you for a seal or something else it eats if it can't see you properly. Also, why would you want to swim in dirty water? That is minging, that is.

4. DO NOT SWIM ALONGSIDE SCHOOLS OF FISH

Sharks are attracted to this sort of thing for obvious reasons.

5. DO NOT WEAR SHINY JEWELLERY

A shark might think it is **fish scales**. You might as well wear a fish costume and swim around singing, 'Come and eat me – I'm so tasty.'

But I think there are some general rules here to learn:

Don't go around looking like someone's dinner.

Don't swim with sharks if you look like **a seal**.

Don't hang around with lions dressed like **a zebra**.

Don't walk across your school playground dressed as **a chicken nugget**.

Collective nouns: Page 148

Shark-attack hotspots around the world: Page 138

Jokes about sharks

I've spent the last year trying to find jokes about sharks. There are loads on the internet and they are all terrible. Mainly they just involve really bad puns about things being **fintastic** or **sharcastic**.

So I have made up some of my own **terrible** shark jokes!

Negative language used to describe sharks: Page 180

Why did the shark cross the road?

Because it was using the Earth's magnetic field to navigate.

How do sharks navigate?: Page 80

How many sharks does it take to change a lightbulb?

Two. One to change the lightbulb and one to silently appear from nowhere at great speed and eat your stepladder.

What's black and white and red all over?

A penguin after having a negative teeth-based rendezvous with a great white shark.

A girl takes her pet shark into school for show-and-tell. Everyone is very impressed. At the end of the day, the shark flops down in the carpet area and goes to sleep. The girl gets her bag ready to go home but her teacher says, 'You can't leave that lyin' in there.' And the girl says, 'That's not a lion — it's a shark.'

Can you keep pet sharks?: Page 150

What's grey and if it lands on your head it'll really hurt?

A police station.

A dead shark landing on your head: Page 89

Different types of shark attack: Page 184

Cheating at swimming races

Retrieving bricks from the bottom of the pool in your pyjamas: Page 186

I have worked out a brilliant way to **win** every single swimming race you ever compete in.

The trick is - **DON'T GET IN THE WATER!**

What I've noticed, you see, is that swimming is a lot **slower** than walking.

NO RUNNING OR PULLING FACES

When everyone else dives in and starts splashing about in the water, simply get off the jumpy-off thing and walk round the edge of the pool while pulling faces.

You will win **every** time.

Whatever you do, do not run around the edge of the pool. Eighty-three people a year die from running beside a pool, slipping over and drowning.

Irrational fear of sharks: Page 98

Hooves!

More people in the world are **killed by horses** every year than by sharks.

So why don't we stop making films about terrifying sharks and make one called **Hooves?** About a human-eating horse!

A great white horse is terrifying riding schools around the countryside. A policeman, a scientist and an old kooky jockey set off in a Range Rover and horsebox to find it!

We're gonna need a bigger horsebox!

It's made a hole in my jodhpurs.

What we are dealing with is an eating machine. All this machine does is trot about, eat and do a poo the size of your head.

Smile, you son of a donkey!

Vending-nado!

Apparently, vending machines kill more people than sharks do. So why doesn't someone make a movie about a guy who owns a vending-machine factory? When a **tornado** hits the town, it picks up thousands of deadly vending machines and starts flinging them in all directions. Our hero must save the world from vending-machine-related disaster.

Jersey Shore Cow Massacre!

Cows kill a lot more people than sharks, too. Why doesn't someone make a movie about a group of hikers being hunted down by milky heifers?

It's got udders! Help me!

There's so much milk. Milk everywhere.

I really hate cows.

Traffic light attack!

Apparently, traffic lights kill a lot more people than sharks. Why doesn't someone make a movie about some sailors stranded in the water after their boat is torpedoed? Little do they know that traffic lights are hunting them from below.

First you hear a faint beeping. Then it gets louder and louder and louder until a little green man leaps out of the ocean and attacks you! But only for ten seconds. Then it flashes for a bit and fades away.

Toffee fudge dolphin

This isn't a shark so it shouldn't be in this book at all but it got in by mistake.

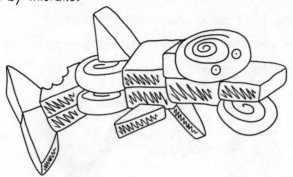

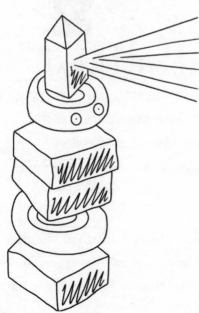

The toffee fudge dolphin is now **extinct** and was probably the most unsuccessful marine creature that has ever existed. Being 90% sugar, they were preyed upon by almost every sea creature out there, and only managed to survive for as long as they did by using various **silly hats** to disguise themselves as lighthouses.

In 1976, a group of old ladies on a coach trip to Budleigh Salterton saw a pod of toffee fudge dolphins and, without a thought for the careful balance of the ecosystem, leaped into the sea and chased after the dolphins until they were all gone.

Little did they know that this was **the last pod** of toffee fudge dolphins, and now they are extinct.

Things that should not be in this book: Page 236

Shark oil: Page 118

Baby Shark

In 2018 a company called Pinkfong (a company – not a band) released a song called 'Baby Shark'.

Before this, the song had been sung by **millions of children** in playgrounds, at camp and on the backs of buses for years but Pinkfong decided to actually record it. It went totally viral, made millions for Pinkfong and pretty much **broke the internet**.

'Baby Shark' is probably one of the **worst songs** ever made. It's also one of the songs that gets stuck into your brain for days and days until you feel that the only way to get it out of your mind would be to train a group of hedgehogs to climb inside your ears, run around in your head and eat the song!

Frugal Sharkish: Page 169

Swimming with sharks: Page 232

Why are sharks endangered?: Page 70

'Baby Shark' follows a noble tradition of bad children's songs which includes:

'The Wheels on the Bus'
'The Crazy Frog'
'I Know a Song that Will Get on Your Nerves'
'Angry Banana'

Blake Chapman

A lot of the actual true facts in this book I have found in a brilliant book called **Shark Attacks**, written by Blake Chapman.

Blake Chapman is an expert on sharks. She did postgraduate research on shark neuroscience, development and ecology, and also worked in aquatic animal health and husbandry.

The aim of her book is to help educate the public on sharks and shark attacks and to better protect sharks and the humans that choose to share their incredible environment.

She can also get a brick from the bottom of a swimming pool in her **pyjamas**.

Thank you, Blake Chapman, for being such an expert.

How to avoid being mistaken for lunch: Page 206

How to defend yourself against a shark attack: Page 188

Lemon meringue pie shark

You've heard of the lemon shark. Well this is the lemon meringue pie shark.

The lemon meringue pie shark has a long tail with which it can whip egg whites to a stiff peak. It can also make a mean pastry.

DeWalt Drill Driver shark

There are plenty of different types of hammerhead shark, so why not have some other sharks that are **named after tools?**

The DeWalt drill driver shark is often mistaken for **a narwhal** because it has a protrusion on the front of its head that it uses for drilling holes in turtles, bolting them together and using them as really terrible bookshelves.

Blender shark: Page 201

Cabbage shark

The cabbage shark is a pale green colour and smells of **dinner ladies**. It is one of the few sharks that is not endangered at all because no one wants to eat it.

Toffee fudge dolphin: Page 216

Famous types of shark: Page 18

Fart-chuckling shark

Almost all sharks propel themselves through the water using their muscular tails and fins.

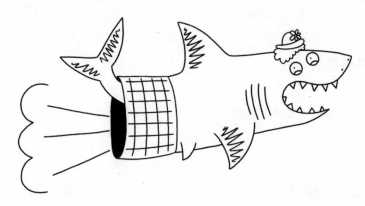

The fart-chuckling shark, however, barely moves its tail at all but gives itself forward motion by producing the most **enormous** and powerful bottom-burps ever seen or smelled.

The main drawback of this is that bigger sharks can smell the fart-chuckling shark from over 160 kilometres away and often swim by to check it out. When threatened by a large shark such as a tiger shark, the fart-chuckling shark simply gives a nervous giggle and farts away with no movement but the gentle **frilling of its bumflaps**.

Things that should not be in this book: Page 236

What you can do to help endangered species

It's all very well knowing about different animals that are endangered because of **humans**.

Why are sharks endangered?:
Page 70

Here are some **suggestions** of what you can do now to help the world:

1. TALK TO YOUR FAMILY

Let your grown-ups know how **important** the planet and endangered species are to you.

Most endangered shark:
Page 108

How sharks do good in the ocean:
Page 154

2. GET INVOLVED WITH YOUR OWN LOCAL WILDLIFE

It's good to be aware of snow leopards in the Himalayas, but what is going on in your **back garden** or the bit of grass near where you live? How many worms are there? Could you be doing more for garden birds? What about bats? And hedgehogs?

3. BE CAREFUL WHAT YOU SPEND YOUR AND YOUR FAMILY'S MONEY ON

Every time you buy something, you are casting a vote as to how you want the world to be.

If you spend money on a plastic toy, you are saying to the world, 'I would like there to be more plastic, please.'

If you spend money on some **organic bread**, you are saying, 'I would like food to be grown without nasty chemicals and with endangered species protected, please.' You could even buy some flour and make your own bread. The **smugness** you will feel is worth millions.

4. DON'T EAT THINGS WITH PALM OIL IN THEM

Palm oil seems to be one of the **worst things** for the environment. Look at the ingredients before you buy food. If it lists palm oil, some of the rainforest has probably been chopped down.

5. PLANT SOME STUFF FOR INSECTS

The world needs bees and wasps and other tiny things we can't even see. Grow flowers in your garden, or on your balcony or window sill, or on top of your hat. Just something with some soil and seeds in it that insects will love.

6. DO NOT BUY ANYTHING WITH PLASTIC PACKAGING

But how does plastic end up in the ocean? Page 132

Plastic is desperately damaging to all wildlife. Learn how to **shop locally**, buy things from farmers directly, maybe even grow some of your own food. It is difficult, especially if you live in a city. But a little bit can go a long way.

7. WRITE TO YOUR MEMBER OF PARLIAMENT AND TELL THEM HOW YOU FEEL

Politicians can make a huge difference but they only think as far ahead as the next election. They are not the right people to look after our planet and our animals. **You are**.

8. VOLUNTEER YOUR TIME

Get **involved** in clearing up woodlands, picking litter out of rivers, building fences, planting trees. Go on a beach clean – you might even find some new Lego! Find out what is going on where you live and **be helpful**.

It's very easy to think that you can't make a difference. But you can. There is enough space on the planet for billions of people to live without wiping out sharks, orang-utans, skylarks, snow leopards and all the other **endangered** creatures.

This book is about sharks, but there are plenty of books about saving the planet. Go and find them. Join the groups. Write the letters. Grow the flowers. If you don't do these things, who will?

Things that aren't in this book much

There are nearly **500 different types of shark**. I didn't have enough pages to write something funny about all of them. Here are some awesome sharks that didn't make it into this book:

Greenland shark; whitetip reef shark; silky shark; sand-tiger shark; spiny dogfish; porbeagle; sandbar shark; dusky shark; six gill shark; zebra shark; Port Jackson shark; squatina; gulper shark; frilled shark; Galapagos shark; kitefin shark; goblin shark; winghead shark.

All of these sharks are brilliant, and when I'm rich I'm going to buy myself an ocean to keep them all in.

Jaws!: Page 34

How do sharks navigate?: Page 80

There are also some things that I've mentioned but would love to write more about.

Famous types of shark: Page 18

I would love to write more about plastics in the ocean and what we can do to clean up and protect our planet. I'd love to write more about some of the other really terrible shark films that are out there. I'd also love to write more about how sharks navigate using electro-reception, lateral line and their ampullae of Lorenzini. But one book can't have everything!

Why is there so much plastic in the sea?: Page 130

If there is anything at all in this book that has made you think, 'Ooh. I would like to know more about that ...' then send me an email at: pleasestopbotheringme@getoutofmyface.org

Or – why don't you go to your local library and read some books about whatever it is you are interested in. They have free books about **everything in the world**.

How to overcome fear

Lots of people are afraid of all sorts of things.

I used to be afraid of swimming in the sea because I thought sharks would eat me. But I faced my fear, and every time I've swum in the ocean since then, the fear has got less and less.

These days, if I feel myself getting a little tummy-wobble when I'm in the waves at Felixstowe, I just have a little **chuckle-fart** to myself about the whole thing.

There's a nice acronym to the word **fear** and it contains its own solution: Face Everything And Recover.

If you have lots of fears, you might want to talk to some grown-ups, read some proper doctor-type books, phone a helpline, all that sort of thing. But **do something** about it.

Whenever I get afraid of something, I try to remember that so far everything has worked out OK. Even though there are sharks out there, and lions and **angry bananas** and giant gorillas, somehow the universe has always kept me safe.

I used to be afraid of sharks. Now I think they are **amazing**. And love them.

If I wasn't already married I would marry a shark. Maybe one day, when the moment is right, I'm going to ask my wife if she could dress up as a shark on Saturdays.

F.E.A.R.

How I got over my phobia of sharks: Page 104

Irrational fear of sharks: Page 98

Fart-chuckling shark: Page 223

Swimming with sharks: Page 232

Swimming with sharks

On 10th October 2019, I did something I never thought I would be able to do. I did a shark dive. I swam with **actual sharks**.

I did my shark dive at Skegness Aquarium in Lincolnshire. It's a fantastic place and you can look at all sorts of fish and sea creatures there. But, very excitingly, you can spend half a day in the water and watch fish and sharks swim around you.

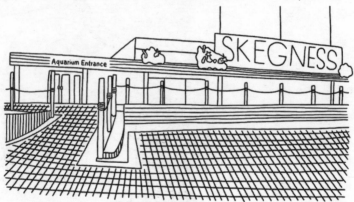

The first thing that happened was we watched a film about sharks and learned about the three different types of shark they have there. There were some blacktip reef sharks, a banded houndshark and a big zebra shark, called **Nudge**.

Next, we got into **wetsuits**, which keep you warm in the water and make you look a bit like a leggy seal. You learn how to use scuba gear. They strap tanks of air to your back and attach weights so you sink to the bottom.

You then practise in a little tank with some **baby sharks**. While I was in there, they fed the babies with bits of fish and it was amazing to see them swimming around my knees chasing the food. They were just like **puppies**.

Then it was time to get in the big tank, full of hundreds of fish and bigger sharks. Most of the big sharks were only four or five years old, so they weren't fully grown and they were still **children** really.

I stood at the bottom and watched sharks circling around me. It was incredible. My favourite was Nudge, the **zebra shark**, who loved nothing more than to swim round my head. He was longer than me but I didn't feel scared or worried at all.

Through all my research for writing this book, I've learned that sharks are **not** the vicious predators I thought they were. I learned that even though there are sometimes accidents, there was really no shark danger to worry about.

But what I learned when I was swimming with sharks was just what **wonderful creatures** they are.

The staff at Skegness Aquarium really know their stuff and made the whole experience really **special** for me. If you love sharks, why not try it yourself?

How I got over my phobia of sharks: Page 104

Baby shark: Page 218

I needed to learn more about sharks: Page 26

How to overcome fear: Page 230

I'M TOTALLY JAWESOME

Things that should not be in this book

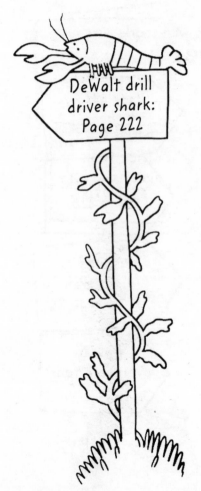

DeWalt drill driver shark:
Page 222

There are lots of things in this book that have absolutely no right to be here. They should be in a different book but they have got into this one by mistake! **Naughty things!**

DeWalt. On page 190, I mention that my preferred choice of weapon against an angry shark would be the DeWalt Brushless 18V Lithium-Ion Keyless Cordless Drill Driver. This is true but I don't actually own one of these drills. I would just really like one. In fact, if I had the whole set, I'd be so happy I'd write about it in all my books.

Television for seals is a very **bad concept**. A seal's life is very busy, filled with fishing, keeping warm and avoiding sharks. To suggest that families of seals have the time to sit around and watch things on the telly is extremely disrespectful to a seal's work ethic.

Shirley Bassey should not be in this book. She should be in some sort of palace for **living treasures**.

Centipede. On page 60, there is an illustration of a centipede saying 'I don't want to be in this book'. Well, if he doesn't want to be in the book, let him go free!

TV shows for seals: Page 38

Who the crumbling plimpturtle is Shirley Bassey?: Page 192

Nice films about sharks: Page 120

Finning. It was important to write about this **terrible practice** but I wish it didn't exist and then I wouldn't have had to mention it. Maybe keep hold of this book after you've read it, stick it in a box in the loft and then when you are grown up and have your own children, you'll take them to granny and grandpa's house and your mum will say, 'Why don't you go up to the loft and get **all those books** – the ones from when you were little. Maybe the children would like to look at them.'

And your children will pick up this book and read it at bedtime. And in the morning, they will say to you, 'There's something called finning in this book. It sounds absolutely **barbaric**. Does that still happen?'

And you will say, 'No. it doesn't happen anymore. But when I was little people killed about 100 million sharks a year, just for their fins. After years of protest and campaigns and books about it, it was eventually banned and now most sharks are protected species and are off the endangered list. They have their rightful place in the ocean and in the world's ecosystem. People **respect** sharks. They are part of our world and we love them.'

I wonder what **other facts** in this book will be no longer true when you are grown-up.

How big are sharks?: Page 60

How to defend yourself against a shark attack: Page 188

The last page of the book

This is the **last** page of the book. Well done for finding it! You get to see a picture of a **naked whale shark.**

It doesn't have to finish here, though. Why not go back and see if you missed anything? Or try reading the book again but this time **upside down while wearing a shark costume.**

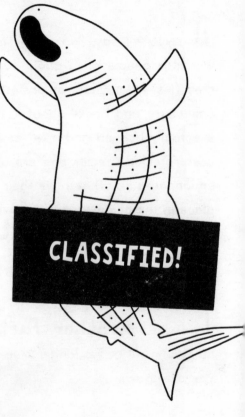

CLASSIFIED!

Beginning page: Page 14

Take a picture and send it to me at: seriouslystopsendingmestupidpictures@ohmycod.com